GRACE MARIE SINCLAIR

CONFIDENCE BOOSTER GUIDE

Unleashing Your Inner Confidence for
Success in Every Area of Life
(2024 Crash Course)

First edition

This book was professionally typeset on Reedsy.
Find out more at reedsy.com

Contents

Confidence Booster Guide

"Elevate Your Essence"
A Step-By-Step Journey to Self-Worth
and
Enhanced Self-Esteem

Introduction

Confidence in oneself is fundamentally rooted in one's self-perception, reflecting a deep sense of personal worth. However, the concept of self-confidence goes beyond mere belief in oneself. It encompasses the ability to navigate life's daily trials and tribulations, understanding that you are likely to experience joy, success, and fulfillment along the way.

Self-confidence is influenced by a multitude of factors, both internal and external. This means that both internal factors, originating within you, and external factors, originating outside of you, can significantly impact your self-perception. Low self-confidence can exert a profound influence on various aspects of a person's life, including family, career, and health. It is essential to learn how to navigate these variables to cultivate self-confidence and preserve a sense of self-worth. True self-confidence resides in trusting yourself and recognizing your inherent worthiness.

However, it's crucial to explore how low self-confidence can impact an individual's life. Self-esteem, which is closely related to self-confidence, flourishes when one feels positive about themselves. Conversely, low self-confidence emerges when negative emotions are associated with oneself or a specific situation. These emotions may stem from experiences like rejection, anxiety, loss, ridicule, or deprivation – the very factors that often erode self-confidence.

Three core elements play a pivotal role in shaping an individual's level of confidence:

1. Values: Understanding and living by your core values is essential for self-appreciation. When your beliefs are clear, you are more likely to appreciate your own existence. Self-respecting individuals are self-aware and confident in their identity.

2. Mastery: Mastery involves being in control of your life and work, leading to greater self-assurance and a heightened sense of importance. Achieving success in your endeavors bolsters confidence and self-worth.

3. Goals: Setting clear objectives is crucial for boosting self-confidence. Pursuing tasks aligned with your desires or beliefs instills a sense of purpose and accomplishment.

It is evident that self-confidence is a multifaceted concept, influenced by various factors that can significantly impact an individual's life. However, by focusing on the positive aspects of life and harnessing your strengths, you can witness an immediate improvement in both your confidence and self-worth.

Low self-confidence affects people of all ages, from children to adults. In adolescents, it often stems from social interactions such as forming friendships in school or family dynamics. Children gauge their self-worth based on perceived external evaluations, making it essential to consider how others perceive them.

In adulthood, self-confidence largely derives from self-assessment and personal accomplishments. Life events like work-related challenges, comparisons with peers, marital status, family, or financial success can positively or negatively impact one's self-confidence. External factors, such as traumatic experiences like breakups or loss, can significantly diminish self-esteem.

Low self-confidence can initiate a destructive cycle leading to depression, even in young children. Feeling worthless hinders individuals from seeking opportunities for personal growth, exacerbating their negative self-perception.

During such challenging times, external support from close friends and problem-solving can aid those with low self-esteem. In mild cases, these individuals often underestimate how others perceive them, as those close to them hold them in high regard.

For severe cases, professional therapy may be necessary to identify the root causes of low self-confidence and provide guidance on improving it. Building self-esteem requires determination and commitment, but the rewards far outweigh the initial challenges.

Self-confidence is a vital aspect of life that propels us toward success. A negative self-perception hinders progress, while self-belief is the key to a positive and fulfilling life.

To cultivate self-confidence, we must maintain a positive and empathetic mindset, serving others and valuing their feelings. Avoid selfishness, as genuine self-worth comes from being a trustworthy and considerate person. Always believe in your capabilities, and refrain from negativity toward others. Radiate warmth and kindness through your actions and expressions, and you'll receive positive responses from those around you, further bolstering your confidence.

Lack of self-confidence leads to introversion and negatively impacts one's life. It can result in sluggishness and a loss of qualities that were once evident. Recognize your strengths and work on your weaknesses. Focus on your strengths, and keep your head held high.

One significant reason for lacking self-confidence is failing to acknowledge one's own abilities. Everyone possesses unique strengths that deserve recognition. Most individuals focus on their shortcomings rather than their strengths.

Another factor contributing to diminished self-confidence can be traumatic events within one's relationships. Some individuals can grow from such experiences, while others become consumed by them. Childhood upbringing can also significantly influence self-confidence. Conflicts between parents or a mother's unrealistic expectations can create self-esteem issues in a child's mind. Families should openly discuss their issues with children and provide guidance to help them build self-confidence.

Chapter 1: Understanding Self-Confidence

Self-confidence is a profound and rational belief in one's own abilities and capabilities. It involves a keen awareness of one's weaknesses as well as a recognition of one's strengths. It's a positive mindset that rests on the conviction that you possess the necessary resources to effectively respond to life's challenges.

The level of your self-confidence is a direct reflection of how you perceive yourself, and it significantly influences how others perceive you. The way people interact with you and react to you is a mirror of your self-perception. When you lack self-confidence, it becomes challenging for others to have confidence in your abilities.

Low self-esteem tends to focus excessively on your flaws and mistakes, essentially making you your own harshest critic.

Individuals who exude self-confidence don't solely depend on the approval of others. While they listen to and value the opinions of others, they ultimately make their own judgments.

Like most individuals, self-confident people set realistic goals, establish concrete objectives, and pursue their dreams. They encounter obstacles along the way, just like everyone else. What sets self-confident individuals apart is how they handle situations when things don't go as planned. They step back, evaluate the situation, and seek the best available options.

When faced with setbacks, they reach a point where they understand that they can't always have things their way. They carry the lessons learned from previous experiences forward, eagerly embracing new goals and dreams. Their unwavering belief in their abilities remains intact, knowing they are now wiser, more knowledgeable, and better equipped with experience.

Let's be clear: self-confidence is not something we are born with. It's not an inherent trait. Self-confidence takes time to develop and requires nurturing. However, it's a quality that anyone can cultivate. Setting the standards and expectations for your own self-confidence is up to you.

Sometimes, people tend to view self-confidence as a magical solution, as if it alone can make all problems disappear. However, self-confidence is just the starting point. To achieve your desired life, you must take action. Success requires perseverance, persistence, logical thinking, trustworthy guidance, and many other factors in addition to self-confidence. Self-confidence is the crucial first step.

When you encounter a self-confident person, you may perceive them as being comfortable in all areas of life. However, self-confidence doesn't encompass everything. Consider the example of Robert Kiyosaki, the author of "Rich Dad Poor Dad." He exudes confidence in his business and entrepreneurial skills, but he openly acknowledges his struggles in academic subjects during his schooling.

Likewise, a friend who is confident in her writing abilities may feel completely out of her element when it comes to working with numbers. Confidence doesn't cover every aspect of life; it has its limitations and areas where it may not apply.

Three Pillars of Self-Confidence

The pursuit of genuine self-confidence often leads us down various paths. We all wish for a quick fix, a magic formula that can instantly transform us into someone with unwavering self-confidence, complete with the attributes and charisma of a self-assured individual. However, self-confidence cannot be attained simply by reading self-help books or attending seminars. It doesn't come from a one-time effort that leaves you disappointed when it doesn't work. Simply envisioning yourself as confident won't make it a reality. True self-confidence is cultivated through continuous learning, consistent practice, and unwavering belief.

The first pillar of self-confidence is education. My initial foray into building self-confidence involved reading books and listening to CDs on the subject. I sought insights from experts who had achieved self-confidence in their respective fields. Books, CDs, and personal experiences laid the foundation for my self-education. A crucial step in this learning process was to narrow my focus to one specific aspect of my life. For example, in my career, which was in sales and marketing, I needed self-confidence. I devoured books on sales techniques and contract negotiations. I sought advice from the most effective sales and marketing leaders on how they handled various situations. It's important to start with a specific area of your life, as self-confidence is a quality that can be applied across all aspects of our lives.

The second ingredient of self-confidence is knowledge through practice, or simply put, taking action. Many of us have been guilty of learning valuable information and then failing to put it into practice. I'm no exception. Confidence comes from engaging in behaviors that bolster your self-assurance. If you're in marketing and struggling with your confidence, ask for the deal. If you're on a date and want to extend the interaction, simply ask for another date. The outcome is not the immediate concern; it's about taking action. Whether the response is a yes or a no, your self-confidence will receive a boost. Receiving a no provides valuable experience for future attempts. Failure is a crucial part of the learning process. Remember this: those with the highest self-confidence in life are often those who have experienced more failures than successes. View failure as a stepping stone toward unwavering self-confidence. True self-confidence arises when you become comfortable with failure because, once you are, your mind will continue to seek opportunities in all aspects of life.

The third pillar is belief. Belief is an intangible force that transcends education and experience. It's a force that, when harnessed, can propel you to unimaginable heights. I'm not referring to blind faith but rather a well-founded, prepared, and optimistic confidence. True belief is attained by taking action in the face of doubt. You'll know when you have genuine belief because the knowledge, experiences, and situations that once filled you with apprehension will now exhilarate you. You'll master emotions that no longer fear failure. Your belief will propel you past the barriers of fear, viewing them not as obstacles but as challenges that can only enhance your growth in the long run.

Remember that all three principles of self-confidence must be consistently practiced and applied. Belief initiates change. Faith demands continual action. Learning without practice is less effective than not learning at all. Without taking action, you won't truly learn. Start incorporating all three pillars into your daily life simultaneously to take the first step toward genuine self-confidence.

How Our Early Years Shaped Us

In the realm of Social Sciences, a specific term often tied to the way our parents raised us is frequently discussed: upbringing. Psychologists have found that "parents' actions significantly influence how children perceive themselves, especially during their formative years." Parents play a pivotal role in nurturing self-confidence during early development, which serves as the foundation for raising well-adjusted adolescents and mature adults.

Imagine growing up in a household with perfectionist family members, individuals burdened by unrealistic expectations. They hold themselves to such high standards that they project these unattainable expectations onto you. It can feel like you're set up for failure from an early age, and the impact on your self-esteem can be profoundly negative. When parents or society set unrealistic standards, it can instill fear that hinders you from reaching your full potential.

Now, picture another scenario where your parents are well-established in their own careers, say as nurses, and they expect you to follow in their footsteps. The notion of pursuing a different profession, perhaps as a painter or a chef, arises, leading to heated debates. They discourage you from exploring your own talents, asserting your independence, and dissuade you by saying, "You're not creative enough; you're better off becoming a doctor!" Parents often have a strong protective instinct and aim to shield their children from life's harsh realities. Their love for their children is unwavering, but the children raised in such an environment seldom make mistakes and consequently rarely learn from them.

The choices you make in friends and role models can also significantly impact your life. Recall how you yearned to belong to the popular crowd during your teenage years. You looked up to the most popular individuals on campus and aspired to be like them. You might have tried to emulate their style, attitude, or even become part of their social circle. As you mature, you realize that becoming your authentic self is far more rewarding than being a mere replica of these individuals.

So, what roles do parents and friends play in nurturing self-confidence?

Parents and friends serve as role models for children. They should set positive examples by demonstrating self-esteem, independent thinking, resilience in overcoming challenges, and, most importantly, self-confidence. They are living proof that you can be successful simply by being yourself.

What if I Lack Confidence in Myself?

The concept of self-confidence, often used interchangeably with self-esteem, revolves around the belief that you can achieve or accomplish certain things. Conversely, a lack of self-confidence is rooted in the belief that you are incapable of being or doing something. The terms "low" or "high," as in "low self-confidence" or "high self-confidence," play a pivotal role in defining this concept. These words have the power to either empower or hinder individuals in their journey to develop self-confidence.

For some, the path to greater success hinges on self-confidence, while for others, it can feel like a never-ending cycle of disappointment. Whether you thrive or struggle can, to some extent, be influenced by your level of self-confidence. Self-confidence doesn't exist in isolation; it's a complex interplay of internal and external factors that manifest as clear signs, indicating whether individuals possess it or not.

If you find yourself among those who lack self-confidence, it's essential to understand that self-confidence can be cultivated. While this book primarily addresses issues related to weak and low self-confidence, it's important to realize that the journey toward self-confidence begins with you.

Indicators of a Lack of Self-Confidence in a Person

1. **The Constant Need for Justification:** When you find yourself always feeling the need to explain or justify your actions, especially after making a mistake, it could be a sign of low self-confidence.

2. **Defensive Responses to Critique:** If you habitually feel compelled to answer or defend yourself against any criticism directed at you, it may indicate a lack of self-confidence.

3. **Overcompensation:** Sometimes, individuals with low self-confidence tend to overcompensate for their perceived shortcomings. They may go to great lengths to prove themselves or gain approval.

4. **Body Language:** Your body language can reveal a lot about your self-

confidence. Slumped shoulders, avoiding eye contact, or appearing closed off can be signs of low self-esteem.

5. **Perfectionism:** Striving for perfection can be a learned trait driven by a lack of self-confidence. You may feel the need to excel in everything you do to compensate for self-doubt.

No one is inherently born with unwavering self-confidence. It's the culmination of years of learning how to interact with the world as an individual. From infancy, you're bombarded with both positive and negative messages about yourself. It's how you interpret these signals that ultimately shapes your level of self-confidence.

A prime example of this is public speaking, often cited as one of the most feared social activities. If you observe someone's public speaking abilities, it can provide insight into their level of self-confidence. Let's consider the context of education and the development of self-confidence in a school setting.

In the early years, from preschool through approximately the fourth grade, many children are eager to please. It's not necessarily because they have unshakable confidence in their knowledge but rather a desire to gain approval. When a teacher poses a question in the classroom, you'll see numerous hands raised at this stage of education. Whether their answer is correct or not, the primary goal is to seek acknowledgment.

As children become more aware of their individual identity, this attitude starts to shift. Typically, those with higher self-confidence are more likely to raise their hands when asked a question. This pattern often continues throughout their lives.

The reason this book asserts that self-confidence is an acquired trait is that even the most awkward young adults can "discover" their abilities in the right circumstances, regardless of their age. Consider the real-life story of Michael Oher, the football player made famous by the Baltimore Ravens and the book and movie "The Blind Side."

Externally, Oher was perceived by many as having zero self-confidence. However, while in high school, he experienced transformative moments that altered his life trajectory, revealing the depth of his self-confidence.

If you or someone you know struggles with low self-confidence, remember that it might seem challenging to build self-confidence, but it's a matter of choosing to learn how to do so. Here are some initial steps: Remind yourself daily that you are capable of achieving anything you desire. With time, this affirmation can lead to genuine self-belief, which you'll project to others.

Identify activities or skills at which you excel and ask yourself, "Why am I good at this?" Try to replicate this approach in other areas of your life. Finally, consider the five indicators of low self-confidence listed here and consciously work to do the opposite of each. Low self-confidence is a condition that can often be improved with self-help initiatives.

Self-Acceptance

Self-acceptance is closely intertwined with "self-image." It's the mental picture you've constructed of yourself, encompassing ideas of your level of goodness, success, talent, happiness, or even perceived flaws and shortcomings. This self-image is an accumulation of experiences throughout your life, heavily influenced by both your achievements and setbacks. To enhance self-acceptance, the initial step involves improving your self-image, which, in turn, necessitates changing the way you perceive yourself.

In addition to improving your self-image, one of the most crucial steps towards self-acceptance is learning to embrace yourself as you are at this very moment, complete with all your imperfections. While it's possible to work on improving some of your flaws and deficiencies, the key is to accept them as part of your current self. Some individuals might perceive themselves as too thin, overweight, too tall, not intelligent enough, or may focus on physical features like large ears or a receding hairline. If you identify with such imperfections, it's vital not to blame yourself—often, these are traits you were born with and have no control over. Perfection is an illusion, and no one is flawless. Remind yourself: "I may not be perfect, but that's perfectly fine. No one is, and I will make the most of what I have." Be your own advocate. Why? Because your overall well-being and success are profoundly influenced by your level of self-acceptance. Without it, true contentment and productivity can be elusive. So, stop striving for perfection and start appreciating yourself as you are. This doesn't mean you shouldn't seek personal improvement—it means you should do so with self-acceptance as your foundation.

Your self-acceptance and self-esteem are often significantly influenced by your friends and acquaintances. You tend to boost your self-acceptance and self-esteem when you believe that others hold you in high regard. Conversely, when you perceive that others have a low opinion of you, your self-perception can suffer. Hence, it's crucial to prevent this from happening. Don't concern yourself with what others think—most of the time, you're the best judge of yourself. However, it's important to remember that no one can make you feel bad about yourself unless you permit it. People sometimes make hurtful comments, often unintentionally (though sometimes deliberately). Don't dwell on them. How you view yourself is ultimately your domain—if you allow it. Train yourself to brush off such remarks.

One of the simplest methods to enhance self-acceptance and confidence is to sit down and list your accomplishments. You may not think you've achieved much, but you might be surprised. Reflect on the milestones you've reached, the accolades you've earned, the years you've dedicated to education, be it school or university. Consider your achievements in your hobbies and interests, and jot them down. When you're done, take pride in these accomplishments and acknowledge them when you talk about them.

Tips on Self-Acceptance

1. **Don't try to impress others.** Instead, focus on being yourself and staying true to your values.
2. **Reflect on the positive aspects of your life.** Take time to appreciate the things you love and the accomplishments you've achieved.
3. **Don't ignore your faults and shortcomings—accept them.** Acknowledge your imperfections and commit to working on them if possible.
4. **Choose a role model—someone you admire—and emulate their positive qualities.** Learn from those you respect and incorporate their best traits into your own character.
5. **Set goals.** The process of achieving goals can boost your confidence and make you feel accomplished.
6. **Avoid apologizing excessively, blaming others, or complaining.** Focus on problem-solving and learning from your experiences.
7. **Learn from your mistakes.** Mistakes are valuable opportunities for growth and self-improvement.
8. **Occasionally revisit your "best moments" in your memory.** Remind yourself of your unique talents and strengths.
9. **Remember that everyone has things they don't like about themselves.** You are not alone in your self-doubts.
10. **If you start worrying about something you don't like about yourself, remind yourself that nobody's perfect.** Accept your imperfections as part of being human.
11. **Take inventory of the things you genuinely enjoy doing and your weaknesses.** Evaluate whether your weaknesses align with your interests and work on improving them if needed.
12. **Reflect on your strengths and weaknesses honestly.** It's not about creating an unrealistic self-image; it's about being genuine with yourself. Analyze your abilities and weaknesses but always emphasize the positive.
13. **Learn from people you respect, but don't try to copy them outright.** Instead, integrate their admirable qualities into your personality.

Self-acceptance and self-confidence are crucial in the workplace, bridging the gap between low self-esteem and healthy self-assuredness. Managing your own self-confidence and encouraging others to do the same is essential. It's evident that many people struggle with low self-confidence, making it vital for leaders and managers to cultivate positive self-confidence within their teams.

Self-confidence empowers individuals to control situations and events rather than being controlled by them. It can help alleviate depression and counter irrational or harmful thoughts, fostering a mindset of "can do" rather than "can't do." Additionally, self-confidence facilitates the pursuit of optimistic performance goals.

Remember, your self-confidence belongs to you alone. While it may face challenges from time to time, you have the power to control and nurture it. Utilize your self-confidence as a tool for outperforming others and staying in control in various situations. Ultimately, your self-confidence is a cornerstone of personal and professional success, so safeguard it and don't let others undermine it.

Individuals at All Levels of an Organization

Individuals occupy various roles within an organization, and social norms, practices, and corporate structures often grant unique privileges to certain entities. These privileges may include specialized expertise, prestigious titles, corner offices, or employee benefits. Consequently, they may hold real or perceived authority or a position of control. What's crucial to recognize is that the power that you believe they hold over you is often given by your own perception and beliefs.

The truth is that everyone enters this world and departs from it in the same way—with their first and last breath. What distinguishes people are the experiences they undergo, how they choose to integrate those experiences, and the paths they forge in their lives. From a personal standpoint, I've come to realize that, irrespective of their position, role, or title, I've encountered individuals with varying levels of self-confidence.

Early in my career, I had the opportunity to develop a personal connection with the company president. On one occasion, we were on a boat at his summer home by a river. I was cautious with my words, responding with "Yes sir, no sir, three bags full sir." However, as we reached the pier and he stepped out of the boat, he playfully pushed me into the water. With a friendly smile, he extended his arm to help me out of the chilly water and told me he liked to have fun just like anyone else. I've never forgotten that lesson, and it instilled a lasting sense of self-confidence in me. I learned how to interact with individuals older and in higher positions than I was. While I treated them with the respect they deserved and still do, I recognized that fundamentally, they are no different from you and me. We all deserve equal respect and recognition for our individuality. Remember that the interactions and communications you have with others on your path to success can significantly impact your learning and the growth of your self-confidence.

Managing Upward – Developing a higher level of self-confidence is crucial for dealing with individuals in higher positions. Understand that they can relate to you just as easily, appreciate your skills, and value your contributions, regardless of their status. It's entirely possible that they themselves may have uncertainties or lack knowledge in certain areas. It's not an unrealistic expectation for leaders to be experts in all domains. Your self-confidence level will enable you to assert yourself comfortably. As you build rapport, your colleagues will come to appreciate your engagement. As their confidence in you grows, they are likely to entrust you with greater responsibilities. There may be times when they cannot accurately assess your skills and personal drive for a specific task. In such cases, it will be up to you to communicate effectively to successfully complete the task. Managing upward is a valuable learning experience that reveals the true confidence and insight within you. Your self-confidence is the source of this strength, and it may well be the key ingredient that opens doors to success. Simultaneously, it sets an example for other employees on how to navigate their roles effectively.

Mentoring Your Boss and Managing Upward

I've made numerous attempts to mentor or guide my boss. I've offered advice on optimizing processes and shared successful solutions from similar situations in the past. One effective approach is simply asking for their opinion on the outcome of a particular matter or how they might have handled it differently. Sometimes, I directly inquire if they are open to alternative approaches and present them with compelling ideas to consider. Over time, with the right level of respect, people often start seeking your input—a truly rewarding experience.

Managing Downward – When you interact with your employees, your self-confidence becomes a signal of their unwavering trust in you as a manager. As your self-confidence rises in addressing challenges, so does theirs. Let it waver, and you'll come under scrutiny. An essential practice is to encourage your employees to brainstorm ideas, especially those that may outshine your own. Encourage them to be at their best and readily accept that some may outperform you one day. Fostering this environment allows them to realize their potential beyond their expectations, and they will be grateful for it. Avoid making assumptions and explaining what people want; this will only limit their exposure to uncharted territories. As a leader, your role is to create an open environment and provide guidance on navigating the vast world before them. What happens when you do this? They have faith in you, you have faith in them, and they gain confidence in themselves. You've ignited a positive momentum that fuels both your performance and theirs!

Moving Through – The same principles apply to interactions with colleagues, whether moving up or down within an organization. You will be observed and assessed. The world is both social and competitive, and individuals with higher self-confidence often stand out among their peers. Gather information and data, maintain a positive outlook, set realistic goals for yourself and others, and seek assistance from those who can positively influence outcomes. In fact, a leadership team with high self-confidence can shape an organization's culture—a culture of confidence! This is a culture that emphasizes encouragement and praise over punishment.

Learning to harness your level of self-confidence and using it positively can be a powerful tool in progressing toward your personal and professional goals. However, a word of caution: ensure you don't mistake unchecked ego for self-confidence, both in yourself and others. I've learned firsthand that effective managers and leaders should be engaged in two ways: nurturing and bolstering their own self-confidence and instilling confidence in those they lead. Leadership effectiveness should not be a reflection solely of the individual, but rather a measure of confidence within the people for whom they are responsible.

Self-Esteem, Self-Confidence, and Self-Efficacy: Understanding the Differences

Frequently, there's confusion between self-esteem and self-confidence. They are not the same, and there are key distinctions between them.

What is Self-Esteem?

Self-esteem is unconditional; you can have full self-esteem just by being alive and healthy. It acknowledges your intrinsic worth as a human being. When a child is born, it can't do anything on its own. It can't clean up after itself, feed itself, or even survive without assistance. Yet, we treasure it, recognizing it as unique and precious. That's it! The innate value is always there, and no one can take it away from you. If you ever feel you have low self-esteem, remember the newborn and how precious and special it is. Then, apply that sense of wonder and gratitude to yourself. You're alive, possessing the power of thought, emotion, expression, and movement. You can do things! This is awe-inspiring, considering the sheer freedom of being alive and having the ability to think, perceive, speak, and act as you wish. Embrace the awe of your natural capabilities and realize how unique and special you are. No one is quite like you. Respect yourself regardless of your actions or identity.

Self-Confidence: Trust in Your Abilities

Self-confidence is the belief that you can perform certain tasks or activities. It's contingent on your skills and achievements. If you are proficient in a particular skill, you can be confident in your ability to perform it. Confidence is linked to your competence in a specific task. Feeling confident without competence is futile. For instance, being confident about skydiving without any experience or knowledge about it is a recipe for disaster. Without competence, confidence can lead to folly. Naturally, your confidence should grow as your skills improve. There's another factor that can boost your confidence in any skill…

Self-Efficacy: The Belief in Your Ability to Learn and Achieve

Self-efficacy is the perception or belief that stems from having confidence in a range of different abilities. As you practice and acquire new skills, your confidence in your ability to learn and achieve grows, and you begin to trust in your own effectiveness. The thought process goes like this: "I've learned to walk, talk, think for myself, drive a vehicle, take care of myself, and add other accomplishments here, so I can learn more. I may not know how to do it right now, but I know how to find someone to teach me, and I know how to invest time and resources in learning a new skill, so yes, I can tackle anything!"

Understanding the distinctions between self-esteem, self-confidence, and self-efficacy can be instrumental in cultivating a strong sense of self and personal development. These elements work together to shape how you perceive yourself and your abilities, ultimately influencing your actions and achievements.

Chapter 2: Overcoming Self-Doubt

I t's evident that conquering self-doubt and fear is one of life's most formidable challenges. Our level of self-confidence greatly impacts the quality of our lives, as anxiety is a peculiar form of internal torment that can easily creep in.

So, how can you conquer the fears, challenges, and anxieties that besiege your thoughts? What can you do to trust yourself more and overcome the self-doubt that hinders your success?

Self-doubt is a common experience, and each of us grapples with it in our own way. Doubt and anxiety are elusive and often deeply ingrained in our minds. A mistake, a setback, or even a minor failure can trigger self-doubt and shake your confidence. Before you know it, trust starts to wane.

Whether you're starting a business or pursuing a dream, self-doubt can creep in as you compare yourself to those who have succeeded before you and feel overwhelmed by the effort required. At this stage, you might even start to believe that you can never achieve the success others have.

However, success lies in having the courage to follow your dreams and stay true to your path, regardless of how different it may be from those who came before you. Understand that self-doubt is not rational behavior, and you can overcome it.

"Self-doubt ruins more dreams than failure ever will." - Suzy Kassem

None of us can ever completely eliminate doubts. Everyone, no matter how successful, grapples with self-doubt at times. But if allowed to take root, self-doubt can become a self-fulfilling prophecy. You may have tried to achieve a goal in the past and decided to give up when faced with a seemingly insurmountable obstacle, but you shouldn't give up.

This is the nature of life! Goals take you out of your comfort zone, push you into new territory, and confront your doubts and fears head-on. The question here is not how to eradicate self-doubt and anxiety but how to make constructive decisions that boost your self-confidence in the face of uncertainties.

Far too many people abandon their aspirations due to self-doubt, insecurity, a loss of faith, or fear.

Moving Beyond Self-Doubt and Fear

Almost all successful individuals openly admit that they grapple with self-doubt on a daily basis. Doubt is so insidious that it has deterred countless people from pursuing remarkable endeavors. However, it's crucial to understand that anxiety does not define you; it's merely a phase you're passing through.

Avoiding uncertainty and anxiety won't make them vanish. Ignoring certain thoughts or looking the other way doesn't make them any less unpleasant or disappear into thin air.

So, take a deep breath. Understand that you still need to take action, even when doubt or deep fear strikes. Don't let paralyzing self-doubt hold you back; instead, take the necessary steps to pursue your goals.

Overcoming Self-Doubt

Eliminating self-doubt on the spot is easier said than done, but here are ways to start conquering self-doubt in order to achieve your desired goals.

Eliminate Negative Language

Begin by erasing words from your vocabulary that sound negative. The phrases, sentences, and verbs you use to describe yourself can significantly impact your self-confidence. Often, these negative words are unfounded.

Instead, cut out or replace words like "never," "still," "can't," "no one," "when," and "will." You'll notice that your mindset and self-doubt can gradually shift for the better.

Recognize Self-Doubt

Identifying self-doubt can be challenging. For example, you might have a fantastic idea to start a business, a website, or even an app. But if you immediately dismiss it with thoughts like "I can't leave my job," or "I have bills to pay," you're succumbing to self-doubt. While there are legitimate concerns, self-doubt can stifle any endeavor. Next time you push an idea away, question whether it's self-doubt or a legitimate concern.

Seek Daily Inspiration

Subscribe to podcasts, watch motivational videos, read books, or watch inspiring movies. Consuming inspirational content can help you address doubts and fears. Seek out thought leaders and mentors, especially when you lack self-confidence.

By adopting these strategies, you can begin to tackle self-doubt and move closer to your goals.

Believe in Your Intelligence

Remind yourself that you are intelligent and capable. Understand that there are individuals in this world who have achieved remarkable feats with fewer resources, skills, incentives, and experiences than you possess. Recognize that you have been successful for others with fewer advantages than you currently have. Often, the biggest obstacle you face is self-doubt.

Reflect on Past Achievements

Consider whether your focus in the morning or throughout the day is on mistakes or on victories. Recent studies suggest that how you remember your past experiences significantly impacts your self-perception and, subsequently, your future actions and outcomes.

Seek Feedback

Seeking feedback from others can be invaluable. Engaging in conversations about your skills and abilities with supportive individuals in your life can help dispel self-doubt. Constructive feedback allows you to see both your strengths and areas for improvement, fostering personal growth.

Beware of Doubt from Others

Dealing with your own self-doubt can be challenging, but the doubts others project onto you can be equally frustrating. As you begin to gain more self-confidence and competence, you may encounter individuals, even those close to you, who project their own self-doubt onto you. They may attempt to discourage your dreams or find reasons why you shouldn't pursue them. Regardless, it's crucial to act on your ideas and goals.

Celebrate Small Wins

When you find yourself trapped in the depths of self-doubt, celebrating small victories can help lift you out. Even if these victories may not seem significant objectively, you can make them meaningful in your mind. Each small step you took to reach that point was a series of incremental actions. Similarly, overcoming self-doubt often requires taking small but essential steps. Celebrating these small wins provides motivation, shows progress, and builds momentum.

Brainstorm Your Path to Success

Take some time to brainstorm events, processes, or initiatives that you believe will lead you to success. This exercise can help you clarify your goals and develop a roadmap for achieving them.

Recognize Your Skills and Learning Abilities

Remind yourself of the skills you already possess and those you can quickly acquire through learning. Recognizing your capabilities can boost your self-confidence and encourage you to take action.

Take Action and Learn

Start putting your skills and abilities into action. Learning by doing can be one of the most effective ways to combat self-doubt. As you see progress and positive results, your confidence will grow.

Believe in Your Capacity to Improve

Believe that you have the capacity to continually improve and do better.

This growth mindset can help you overcome self-doubt and embrace challenges as opportunities for growth.

Find Inspiration and Focus on Results

Seek inspiration from various sources and concentrate on actions that yield tangible results. When you focus on meaningful actions, it becomes easier to stay motivated and avoid self-doubt.

Take Small Steps Toward Progress

Counteract self-doubt by taking small, manageable steps that contribute to overall progress. Breaking down your goals into smaller tasks can make them feel less overwhelming.

Activate Your Inner Genius

Harness your inner creativity and intellect while disregarding self-doubt and external criticism. Trust in your unique abilities and insights.

Use Skepticism as Motivation

When others doubt your abilities or belittle your goals, use their skepticism as motivation to prove them wrong. Let their doubts fuel your determination to succeed.

Choose Your Thoughts Carefully

Be selective about the thoughts you entertain, as they shape your beliefs and actions. Avoid letting others' opinions and your own self-doubt influence your vision and willingness to take action.

Presume Success

Embrace an attitude of success, and don't allow self-doubt to creep in. Recognize that doubts, worries, and uncertainties are natural but choose not to let them hinder your progress.

Overcoming self-doubt requires a proactive mindset and the willingness to take action despite the doubts that may arise. By focusing on your goals, believing in your abilities, and choosing to dismiss self-doubt, you can move closer to what you want to achieve. Life is too short to let self-doubt hold you back from pursuing your aspirations.

Self-Doubt: Its Origins and How to Defuse It

Self-doubt can be traced back to two types of negative anticipations: first, the belief that achieving the goal itself may not be possible, and second, the perception that even if the goal is attainable, you may not be able to achieve it.

To combat self-doubt effectively, you can follow a two-step process:

Stage 1: Recognize That Achieving the Goal Is Not Impossible

Inside your mind, there is constant "self-talk" happening. On one side, there's the part of you that sees endless possibilities, while on the other, there's a critical voice that sets the bar low and convinces you that the goal isn't truly achievable.

Many people go through life without even realizing this internal dialogue is taking place. They may wonder why they are sometimes motivated to take action and at other times not. To overcome self-doubt, you must take full control of this inner conversation and become aware of its influence.

Begin by looking at the situation objectively, removing yourself from the equation. Instead of pondering what you can or cannot do, focus on the goal itself and acknowledge that someone, somewhere on Earth, has achieved or is achieving it. Practice a phrase that breaks the habit of thought that makes you doubt your ability to reach your goal.

For example, if your goal is to achieve financial independence within 12 months, say something like, "It's not difficult to become financially independent within 12 months or less. It has been done repeatedly." This choice of words is deliberate, as it eliminates the opportunity to introduce doubt with phrases like "It's possible, but…"

This is not about positive thinking but realistic thinking, focusing on facts rather than emotions. By removing personal anxiety from the equation and recognizing your capabilities as a human being, you can reframe your beliefs about what is achievable.

Once you've logically presented the goal in your mind and firmly believe it is not impossible, you can proceed to the next stage.

Step 2: Recognize That You Can Achieve the Goal, Especially You

Many individuals stumble at this stage, saying, "Yes, it's possible, but not for me." This is where excuses come into play, where challenges seem insurmountable, and we see ourselves as relatively powerless.

In reality, we possess tremendous power. When we dwell on our limitations, be it energy, finances, skills, or anything else, we relinquish control to that inner voice telling us, "You can't do it." This part of us compiles an exhaustive list of all the reasons why we're not up to the task, and it can be difficult to counter.

The key is to shift the balance and create a clear list of all the reasons why you can do it and why you are uniquely qualified for the task. This is not mere self-promotion; it's a deep reflection on why you are more than capable. It's akin to preparing a compelling case for a job interview, where you outline your qualifications, training, experience, and, most importantly, your achievements.

Imagine presenting this case to a hiring manager and hoping they say, "This person is the perfect fit for the job." Creating a resume for yourself should evoke the same sense of confidence.

To accomplish this, you must set aside time for introspection and do it thoroughly. You need to boast about yourself and acknowledge all the knowledge you've taken for granted. You possess all the tools you need, and you have a wealth of experiences to draw from.

Right now, you may not fully grasp your capabilities because your focus has shifted towards your perceived failures and weaknesses. But it's time to turn the tide.

Now, you must take action.

This is the critical part if you want to conquer self-doubt permanently. Implement this advice, and you will see immediate progress. If you're hesitant to do it now and think, "Maybe it's possible for others, but not for me," bookmark this post and revisit it daily. Eventually, you'll grow tired of your own excuses and choose to act.

Abraham Maslow suggests that building self-esteem is rooted in the core of psychological health, achievable only when an individual's innermost essence is genuinely understood, loved, and respected by both themselves and others. Jack Canfield aptly states, "Self-esteem is about feeling lovable and worthy."

Self-esteem is closely tied to self-image, representing how an individual perceives themselves mentally. Our self-images develop in early childhood, encompassing our strengths, weaknesses, talents, and feelings. These mental representations are reinforced by memories and interactions with others, shaping our self-esteem over time. Self-esteem is influenced by both external factors, such as how others accept and appreciate us, and internal factors, including our self-recognition, self-support, and self-praise. It's the synthesis of these variables that forms our self-esteem, ultimately influencing how we view ourselves and our attributes. In the words of Stanley Coppersmith, a prominent scholar in the field, self-esteem is the "personal judgment of worthiness reflected in an individual's attitudes toward themselves," with high self-esteem implying that we possess enough self-confidence to not rely on external validation.

How is Self-Esteem Developed?

Self-esteem is shaped by a complex interplay of emotions, relationships, and experiences throughout a person's life. Its development begins as early as childhood and continues into late adolescence. Several factors influence the formation of self-esteem:

1. **Internal Feelings and Beliefs:** A person's own thoughts and beliefs about themselves play a significant role in self-esteem. If an individual does not see themselves as possessing the values they admire, it can lead to low self-esteem.
2. **Social Interactions:** How others react to an individual, including family, friends, colleagues, and peers, can impact their self-esteem. Positive interactions and recognition from others can boost self-esteem, while negative interactions can erode it.
3. **Educational and Work Experiences:** Successes and failures in school and career can influence self-esteem. Achievements can boost confidence, while setbacks can lower it.
4. **Health and Well-being:** Physical health, illness, and experiences like recovering from an accident or overcoming a serious illness can affect self-esteem.
5. **Personal History:** Past experiences, including childhood upbringing, trauma, and significant life events, contribute to a person's self-esteem.
6. **Faith and Belief Systems:** A person's religious or spiritual beliefs can shape their self-esteem.
7. **Social Status:** An individual's position and status in society can also impact how they view themselves.

It's worth noting that individuals with low self-esteem may possess qualities and accomplishments that others admire, but they may struggle to recognize their own worth due to conditioned self-images.

According to Dr. Michael Miller, editor-in-chief of the Harvard Mental Health Letter, self-esteem can emerge from clear self-understanding, recognizing one's true talents, and finding joy in supporting others.

The Value of Self-Esteem

Self-esteem is of paramount importance in a person's life, influencing their success and well-being. Brian Tracy emphasizes that self-esteem is a foundational aspect of character, affecting one's achievements in nearly every aspect of life.

A healthy level of self-esteem empowers individuals to:

- Feel confident in pursuing their goals.
- Perform well in various situations.
- Recognize their own worth and feel valued.
- Experience pride in their achievements and themselves.

Individuals with low self-esteem may feel inadequate and may not perform at their best in various situations. They often hold inaccurate beliefs about not being accepted or appreciated by others.

In contrast, those with healthy self-esteem enjoy life more fully, believing they deserve happiness. This belief shapes their interactions with others, fostering positive relationships while avoiding destructive ones. Low self-esteem can lead to unhappiness, underachievement, and acceptance of unhealthy situations and relationships. Additionally, it has been linked to stress, depression, and anxiety.

Research supports the positive effects of healthy self-esteem, including increased life satisfaction, humility, resilience, and confidence. In summary, self-esteem plays a crucial role in nearly every aspect of life, influencing an individual's actions and perceptions.

In the year 2000, the World Health Organization emphasized the significance of improving the self-esteem of children and adolescents in their publication "Preventing Suicide." They highlighted that enhancing self-esteem is crucial to protecting young individuals from mental distress and despair, enabling them to effectively cope with challenging and stressful life situations.

Candito, in the book "Alcoholism: A False Stigma: Low Self-Esteem the

Real Problem" (1996), reported insights from individuals who identified themselves as 'recovered alcoholics.' They stated that low self-esteem was the most significant issue in their lives, and alcoholism was a consequence of this underlying problem.

Glenn R. Schiraldi, Ph.D., author of "The Self-Esteem Workbook" and a professor at the University of Maryland School of Public Health, noted that individuals with healthy self-esteem can assess their abilities, shortcomings, and potential in a realistic and honest manner.

Furthermore, Madelyn Swift emphasized that emotional health is closely tied to self-esteem. Emotional well-being relies on the pillars of self-acceptance and feeling capable.

Developing a healthy self-esteem is crucial, but it's important to acknowledge that many individuals struggle with low self-esteem. According to a study published by the American Psychological Association, self-esteem tends to be lowest in young adults, increases during adolescence, peaks around age 60, and then begins to decline. The study, which assessed 3,617 U.S. adults' self-esteem, found that women, on average, had lower self-esteem than men during most of adulthood. However, self-esteem levels converged as both men and women entered their 80s and 90s. Interestingly, during young adulthood and middle age, there was no significant difference in self-esteem between black and white participants.

Ulrich Orth, PhD, the lead author of the study, emphasized the importance of understanding how the self-esteem of the average person changes over time, as self-esteem is linked to better health, reduced criminal behavior, lower levels of depression, and greater life achievement.

Your emotions play a central role in your self-esteem, and you have the power to influence these emotions. Dwelling on your failures and shortcomings can contribute to low self-esteem. Counteracting such thoughts by focusing on your positive qualities and attributes is a step toward building healthier self-esteem.

Your self-esteem in the present is not merely about how you feel about yourself today but how you fundamentally perceive yourself in the long term. It's important to recognize that childhood experiences have a significant impact on self-esteem. Positive experiences based on affection, trust, and security can foster healthy self-esteem, while negative experiences such as constant humiliation, insults, and lack of positive attention can make it challenging to develop a healthy self-esteem. Even subtle negative or positive experiences during childhood can have a lasting influence on self-esteem.

Arguing with your "inner voice" is a powerful technique for improving self-esteem. We all have that inner monologue that constantly comments on our actions and thoughts. For those with healthy self-esteem, this inner voice often provides reassurance and rewards. However, for individuals with poor self-esteem, it tends to be critical, self-sabotaging, and discouraging.

For instance, if you participate in a competition or attend a job interview and receive a compliment, your inner voice might respond with self-doubt, saying something like, "They were just being nice; you did poorly, don't bother trying next time." To combat this, you should challenge your inner voice and respond with positivity, such as saying, "They praised me because I did well, maybe I wasn't perfect, but win or lose, I gave it my best effort, and I'm proud of myself." Engaging in this inner dialogue and arguing with your inner critic can significantly improve self-esteem. Remember, you are the manager of your thoughts, and you have the power to control your inner dialogue and build a more positive self-image.

Another technique to boost self-esteem is to use negative affirmations, which are essentially positive statements about yourself. Repeating these affirmations to yourself daily, ideally during moments of relaxation or meditation, can be incredibly effective. Here are some examples of positive self-esteem affirmations:

1. Who you are: "I am great. I am good. I am unique."
2. Who you're going to be: "I can be a champion. I can be powerful. I will recover. I will lose weight."
3. What you're going to do: "I'm going to smile more. I'm going to control my emotions."

By constantly repeating these affirmations to yourself, you reinforce positive beliefs about who you are and what you can achieve, leading to improved self-esteem.

Self-nurturing is another essential aspect of boosting self-esteem. This involves taking care of your physical and emotional well-being. Ensure you eat healthily, stay active, and get enough rest. Self-nurturing is about treating yourself as though you are worthwhile. Reward yourself with enjoyable activities, especially after achieving something positive. Acknowledge and appreciate the things you love about yourself, and don't dwell on failures or punish yourself for them. Instead, reward yourself for your efforts and focus on the positive aspects of your life.

On days when you're not feeling your best, make an effort to do things that are good for your well-being, no matter how small they may seem. Seek support and encouragement from loved ones, and let them know what you appreciate about yourself. Sharing your feelings with them and having them listen can significantly boost your self-esteem.

Community and relationships play a crucial role in self-esteem. While not everyone may have a loving partner or a strong community network, it's important to ensure that the people in your life respect you for who you are, and you should do the same for them. Understanding and accepting that people have their differences can help build stronger relationships. Connect with those you encounter daily, communicate, show love, listen, be helpful, and be honest. Recognizing that others see value in you can be a significant self-esteem booster.

Handling criticism effectively is a crucial skill for building and maintaining self-esteem. Here are some tips for managing criticism in a way that supports your self-esteem:

1. **Pause and Reflect**: When you receive criticism, take a moment to pause and reflect on what's being said. Don't rush to apologize or react immediately. Give yourself time to process the feedback.

2. **Assess Validity**: Consider whether the criticism is valid. Is there truth in what the person is saying? If the criticism has merit, acknowledge it and express your agreement with the critic. This demonstrates maturity and a willingness to learn and improve.

3. **Stand Up to Unfair Criticism**: If you believe the criticism is unfair or unjustified, don't hesitate to stand up for yourself. Just as you would challenge your inner critic, respectfully challenge external criticism that you believe is unwarranted.

4. **Listen Actively**: Be an active listener when receiving feedback. Make an effort to fully understand the perspective of the critic. This can help you respond more effectively and demonstrate that you value their input.

5. **Respond Thoughtfully**: Responding to criticism doesn't mean reacting emotionally. A composed and self-possessed individual will calmly listen to feedback and then provide a thoughtful response. Avoid getting defensive or confrontational.

6. **Choose the Right Time**: When offering criticism to others, choose an appropriate time and place. Be considerate of the other person's feelings and be tactful in your delivery. Avoid using accusatory language and focus on "I" statements rather than "you" statements.

7. **Address Issues Promptly**: Don't let annoyances fester. Address issues as they arise rather than letting them escalate. Nipping problems in the bud can prevent them from becoming larger conflicts.

Remember that handling criticism is a skill that can be developed over time. By pausing, assessing, and responding thoughtfully to feedback, you can effectively manage criticism and maintain your self-esteem.

The relationship between environmental factors and self-esteem is a complex and intertwined one. Self-esteem is indeed an internal evaluation of oneself, but it is profoundly influenced by external factors and the environment in which an individual lives. Let's delve deeper into the interplay between these two:

1. **Environmental Impact on Self-Esteem**: Positive environments that promote personal growth, self-confidence, and well-being can significantly enhance an individual's self-esteem. These environments provide opportunities for success, positive feedback, and a sense of belonging. For example, a supportive family, encouraging friends, and a nurturing educational or work environment can boost self-esteem.

2. **Achievement and Self-Esteem**: Accomplishments in one's environment, such as academic achievements, career success, or personal goals attained, contribute to a sense of competence and self-worth. When individuals excel in their chosen environments, it often leads to higher self-esteem.

3. **Social Interactions**: The quality of social interactions in an individual's environment plays a crucial role in shaping self-esteem. Positive interactions with friends, colleagues, and mentors who provide affirmation and validation can bolster self-esteem. Conversely, negative or toxic relationships can erode self-esteem.

4. **Financial and Material Factors**: Financial stability and access to resources can influence self-esteem. Economic hardships or lack of basic needs can contribute to feelings of insecurity and low self-esteem. Conversely, financial success and stability can enhance self-esteem.

5. **Physical Environment**: The physical surroundings, such as living conditions and access to nature and recreational spaces, can impact emotional well-being and self-esteem. A safe, comfortable, and aesthetically pleasing environment can foster positive emotions and self-esteem.

6. **Cultural and Societal Factors**: Cultural norms, societal expectations, and discrimination can influence how individuals perceive themselves. A supportive and inclusive cultural and societal environment promotes healthy self-esteem for all individuals.

7. **Personal Choices and Actions**: While external factors have a significant impact, individuals also have agency in shaping their environments. They can make choices and take actions to create a more positive and

supportive environment that fosters self-esteem.

In summary, self-esteem is not solely an internal construct but is intricately linked to the external environment. Positive environments that encourage personal growth, offer opportunities for success, and provide supportive social interactions can enhance self-esteem. Recognizing the role of environmental factors in self-esteem allows individuals to make intentional choices to create a nurturing and empowering environment that promotes their well-being.

Your exploration of the relationship between environmental factors and self-esteem, as well as the importance of social acceptance and supportive relationships, is insightful. Here are some key takeaways from your text:

1. **The Role of Acceptance and Loving People**: After undergoing a change in their social environment, individuals often need to be accepted and surrounded by loving and supportive people. While family support is crucial, there comes a point in life when dignity, autonomy, and prestige require the validation and respect of others outside immediate relatives.

2. **The Value of Diverse Relationships**: The "others" who contribute to our self-esteem can be friends, colleagues, or even strangers. Building and nurturing relationships with a variety of people can provide different perspectives and forms of support, contributing to improved self-esteem.

3. **The Pursuit of an Ideal Social Circle**: It's essential to recognize that achieving the perfect social circle may be an ongoing process. People should not rush or become anxious but continue seeking connections and relationships that align with their values and contribute positively to their self-esteem.

4. **The Need for Goals and Purpose**: Beyond financial stability, a comfortable living environment, and good company, individuals require meaningful goals and a sense of purpose in their lives. Without these elements, they may experience unhappiness and a lack of fulfillment.

5. **The Power of Changing One's Environment**: In some cases, signif-

icant improvements in self-esteem can only be achieved by changing one's environment, especially if it involves moving to a different culture or location. This step can lead to better opportunities, increased wealth, and enhanced self-satisfaction.

6. **The Importance of Self-Understanding**: Understanding one's fundamental needs and whether they require environmental changes or personal adjustments is essential. Self-awareness helps individuals determine the most effective path to improving their self-esteem.

7. **The Challenges of Self-Improvement**: Achieving higher self-esteem, especially for adults, can be a challenging endeavor. It requires emotional strength, decision-making capacity, and the ability to adapt to various circumstances. Seeking positive examples and guidance is vital in this process.

8. **Resilience and Self-Esteem Maintenance**: Learning how to preserve and boost self-esteem despite external limitations is a crucial skill. It involves developing resilience and coping mechanisms to navigate challenges that cannot be changed.

9. **Continuous Learning and Improvement**: The journey to higher self-esteem is ongoing. There is a wealth of literature and resources available to help individuals understand the principles of self-esteem and apply them in their lives.

Your essay highlights the multifaceted nature of self-esteem and the intricate relationship between personal development, social interactions, and the environment. It underscores the importance of self-awareness, resilience, and a proactive approach to nurturing self-esteem throughout one's life.

Your emphasis on the need for educational programs and curriculum that address self-esteem issues and provide practical solutions is highly valuable. Here are some key points from your text:

1. **Educational Programs for Self-Esteem**: Creating television series or school curricula dedicated to teaching children about self-esteem is a

proactive way to equip them with essential life skills. These programs should go beyond theoretical knowledge and provide practical examples and solutions.

2. **Real-Life Scenarios**: Incorporating real-life scenarios and examples into children's education can help them recognize situations that may lead to low self-esteem. By discussing and dissecting these scenarios, children can gain a deeper understanding of the factors influencing self-esteem.

3. **Problem-Solving Approach**: The educational content should not only highlight the challenges associated with self-esteem but also offer specific solutions. This problem-solving approach can empower children to address self-esteem issues effectively.

4. **Modification of Environment**: Teaching children how to modify their environment to enhance self-esteem is a valuable skill. This involves helping them recognize when environmental changes are needed and how to navigate such changes.

5. **Understanding the Self-Esteem Battle**: The concept of self-esteem as an ongoing battle between one's true self, ideal self, and environmental perceptions is a thought-provoking perspective. Understanding this internal struggle can motivate individuals to continually strive for higher self-esteem.

6. **Lifelong Journey**: Recognizing that self-esteem is a lifelong journey is essential. It implies that individuals should continually seek opportunities for personal growth and self-improvement, even into adulthood.

7. **Preventing Self-Esteem Crises**: By providing children with the tools and knowledge to manage self-esteem challenges, educational programs can help prevent crises and equip them with resilience and coping strategies.

Your ideas underscore the importance of proactive and practical education in shaping children's understanding of self-esteem. By integrating these concepts into their learning experiences, children can develop the skills and mindset needed to navigate the complexities of self-esteem throughout their lives. Additionally, your perspective on self-esteem as an ongoing battle aligns with the idea that personal growth is a continuous journey.

CHAPTER 3: Fostering Genuine Self-Confidence

Inaction tends to breed fears and anxiety, while action nurtures trust and courage. If you wish to conquer apprehension, refrain from simply contemplating it. Instead, take action and get started." - Dale Carnegie

I've spent nearly four decades engrossed in reading, researching, studying, and embodying the principles of positive living. These principles are timeless, universal, and applicable to all. However, I've noticed that one crucial aspect is often underestimated, scorned, misrepresented, or misunderstood—the principle of self-confidence.

The concept of self-confidence has been twisted and redefined into various notions, none of which capture its true essence. It has been labeled as "Self-Centeredness" and sometimes misconstrued as a pursuit of narcissistic self-satisfaction. It's seen as an inflated ego, and some mistakenly believe that confident individuals trample on others to advance. Self-confidence is often misconceived as a lack of genuine ability, replaced by an aggressive and arrogant demeanor that alienates others.

It's imperative for successful individuals to recognize that these negative conceptions of self-confidence are fallacious. In reality, authentic self-confidence is not merely a desirable trait but a prerequisite for success. Without it, we lack the courage to forge ahead, attempt new endeavors, and push our boundaries. A deficiency in self-confidence contributes to the prevailing apathy among many in today's society.

Have you struggled to manifest your dreams? Do you believe you have untapped potential, yet find it challenging to unleash? Few impediments to success are as crippling as a lack of self-confidence in any facet of life. To attain this vital trait, you must first comprehend what it entails and how to cultivate it.

"Every success story I've ever encountered has one common thread: 'My life turned around when I began believing in myself.'" - Dr. Robert Schuller

Self-confidence is the recognition and realization of your unique abilities and potential. It entails understanding what you are capable of and the determination to execute tasks with excellence to the best of your abilities.

Authentic self-confidence does not entail believing you are superior to others; instead, it involves acknowledging that you can achieve remarkable feats.

Contrary to the misconception that self-confidence requires a large ego, true self-assurance is characterized by composure and inner balance. Those with genuine self-confidence pursue their endeavors with precision, without the need to broadcast their achievements to the world. Observers invariably recognize their excellence. It is those lacking self-confidence who feel compelled to trumpet their accomplishments to those around them.

Being self-assured means recognizing that you possess the potential to succeed in specific areas of life while acknowledging that others may excel in different domains. Confident individuals are unthreatened by this fact; instead, they celebrate it. They take pleasure in their pursuits while appreciating the achievements of others. It is the absence of self-confidence that breeds insecurity and competitiveness. A lack of self-assurance leads people to believe they must always outshine others, resulting in frustration and discord. We have witnessed this scenario far too often, and it is never a pretty sight.

Writer Marcus Garvey once stated, "Without self-confidence, you will falter in the journey of life." Believing in your abilities is not a matter of pride or self-centeredness; it's about striving for excellence in your endeavors. Why should you aim to be the best? Not to diminish others or boast, but to offer your utmost because it's a responsibility you owe to others. Giving anything less is both selfish and lethargic.

Dwight D. Eisenhower and Helen Keller, two individuals who faced extraordinary challenges, emphasized the importance of optimism and trust in achieving success. Eisenhower asserted that optimism is the driving force behind accomplishment, emphasizing that nothing can be achieved without hope and trust. Trust, in essence, is the foundation upon which we can build our lives.

Confidence empowers you to confront and tackle the hurdles before you. It's the belief in your ability to reach your goals, even if you encounter difficulties along the way. Confident individuals possess the resilience to persevere, even in the face of formidable challenges.

Abraham Lincoln, a man of profound self-confidence, faced setbacks and disappointments in diplomacy. However, he remained resolute in his belief that he could contribute to his country's betterment. He recognized the importance of surrounding himself with the best leaders of his time, even if they were his rivals. His confidence was not rooted in a sense of superiority but in his unwavering determination to work diligently, especially when faced with adversity. He famously said, "I will prepare, and my chance will come." Success doesn't come because you think you're better or because you believe it's your time; it arrives when you are prepared for it.

The Boy Scouts of America motto, "Be prepared," underscores the importance of readiness. It's not about waiting for opportunities to come to you or assuming you deserve them. Rather, it's about being prepared for whatever challenges or opportunities may arise. Confidence enables us to think clearly and decisively, eliminating endless hours of doubt and hesitation. With self-confidence, it's not a matter of "if" but "when." Those who think in terms of "when" they will have their opportunity and "if" they will face challenges are continually prepared and aware of their life's unfolding events. This self-assurance strengthens with each success, creating a self-perpetuating cycle of growth and achievement.

Myths About Developing Self-Confidence

Individuals who exude self-assuredness and believe in their ability to navigate life's challenges are often a magnet for others. Their self-confidence and poise are evident, making people feel at ease and secure in their presence.

However, there are numerous myths circulating about self-confidence that can mislead many individuals, preventing them from realizing their full potential.

1. **Myth: Self-confidence is an innate trait.** Many mistakenly believe that self-confidence is something you're born with, an unchangeable attribute. This couldn't be further from the truth. Self-confidence, like any skill, can be cultivated with guidance and practice.
2. **Myth: External factors like appearance and education determine self-confidence.** Some individuals blame their lack of self-confidence on their appearance or educational background. However, these external

factors are not linked to self-confidence. It's a matter of belief in oneself, not external characteristics. Building self-confidence begins with self-trust, regardless of appearances or education.

3. **Myth: Self-confidence is directly tied to life's approval and validation.** While approval and encouragement from others can boost one's self-esteem, relying solely on external validation is a flawed approach. True self-confidence comes from within and is earned through one's actions and self-belief. Both successful and unsuccessful individuals can earn respect through their efforts and self-assuredness.

4. **Myth: Only children possess unwavering self-confidence.** It's a common misconception that children naturally possess self-confidence, allowing them to attempt new challenges without fear. In reality, no one is born with all the necessary skills. Children, too, learn and acquire skills over time. The key is nurturing self-confidence early on, which empowers them to explore new endeavors with enthusiasm.

5. **Myth: Only self-confident people can face opportunities.** While self-confident individuals may approach opportunities with more optimism, it doesn't mean that only they can seize chances. People with low self-confidence often fear failure and seek constant approval, hindering their ability to embrace new challenges. Building self-confidence empowers individuals to confront opportunities with courage, learn from setbacks, and grow in the process.

What's clear is the prevalent misunderstanding regarding self-confidence. It's crucial for individuals to recognize that self-confidence is a state of mind, independent of one's physical attractiveness or external presence. It originates from an individual's self-belief, and it can be nurtured and built upon.

All that's required is for individuals to dispel the myths that acquiring self-confidence is an insurmountable challenge or that it's only attainable through exceptional intelligence, talents, or luck. Once these myths are debunked, individuals will find it more accessible to cultivate the same magnetic qualities that self-confident people exude.

Building Self-Confidence: Physical Aspects

Now that we understand what self-confidence entails and its importance, let's explore how to cultivate self-confidence in our lives. It's true that some individuals seem naturally inclined towards a self-confident attitude, while others find it challenging to develop confidence in any aspect of life. Nevertheless, it's essential for everyone to work on their self-confidence levels to achieve their goals.

Self-confidence is an internal power that must be harnessed and controlled, much like other emotions such as anger, love, hate, excitement, and fear, which can be both beneficial and detrimental if left unchecked. These emotions are akin to fire; when controlled and used wisely, they provide warmth, cook food, and generate energy. However, when uncontrolled and misused, they can lead to devastation, as fire has the potential to destroy towns and take lives. Similarly, uncontrolled self-confidence can result in selfishness, arrogance, and emotional turmoil. Properly managed self-confidence, on the other hand, leads to success, service to others, and a fulfilling life.

There are two distinct areas where we can intentionally and effectively build self-confidence: the physical and mental realms.

Building Self-Confidence: Physical

William Hazlitt once stated, "The more we do, the more we can do." Tony Robbins, a renowned motivational speaker, teaches a valuable lesson: "Motion creates emotion."

How we move and act has a profound impact on our thoughts and self-perception. This is a powerful reality for those who understand and apply it, influencing their health, behavior, and attitudes.

One of my favorite pastimes is observing people in public spaces. It's as if God must take delight in His creation, as there's endless fascination in watching human interactions. One striking aspect is how individuals carry themselves. Those who are burdened by life often appear slouched, walk slowly, and avoid eye contact, sometimes wearing a frown to deter social interaction.

Conversely, those who exude confidence and a positive outlook tend to walk with an upright posture, move briskly, and wear a smile. They project an air of contentment with their presence.

Here's an experiment for you to try. Find a comfortable seat, recline with your head down, slow your breathing, and gaze at the floor. Allow the muscles in your face to relax, forming a frown. After a few moments, take note of the following:

1. How do you feel?
2. Are your thoughts predominantly positive or negative?
3. Do you feel happy or sad?

Now, sit up straight, maintain steady eye contact, take deep breaths, and put on a big smile, as if you were Peter Pan. Place your hands on your hips and exude confidence. Ask the same questions again:

1. How do you feel now?
2. Are your thoughts more positive or negative?
3. Do you feel happier or sadder?

Many people will discover that good posture and confident behavior make them feel and appear their best, think positively, and perform at their peak.

Observe successful individuals you encounter. How do they carry themselves? What gestures do they employ when they speak? These are cues for success. By studying and emulating confident and accomplished individuals, you can gain valuable insights into achieving self-confidence and success.

Becoming a more confident individual doesn't happen by chance; it requires a deliberate effort and a keen focus on your actions. Start by asking yourself: "If I were the productive and confident person I aspire to be, how would I carry myself? How would I breathe, speak, make eye contact, and introduce myself?" It might feel somewhat artificial initially, but that's precisely the point. Practice it before you truly embody it. This concept formed the basis of Dale Carnegie's theory of public speaking. He advised his students to act the part before they could become it. You'll discover what feels right for you. If you don't act on it until you believe it, you'll remain where you are. The choice is always yours.

"Believe in yourself! Trust in your abilities! You cannot be successful and happy without a confident, yet reasonable belief in your own powers." - Dr.

Norman Vincent Peale

It's true that how you carry yourself, your appearance, and your actions play a significant role in developing self-confidence. However, the true battleground for self-confidence is your mind. Confidence in oneself is fundamentally about what you feel, how you behave, and what you genuinely believe to be true. Without the right mindset, nothing else will endure. While the physical and emotional aspects of self-confidence are interconnected, the key to genuine self-confidence lies in your mindset.

Have you ever considered what dominates your thoughts? It may seem like an unusual question, as most people rarely discuss their inner thoughts. Yet, many carry around negative and anxious thoughts and wonder why they are not content. They dwell on potential failures in life and ponder why they feel fearful and despondent. They fixate on the effort required to succeed and question why they fall short of their goals. Take a moment to reflect: "What occupies my thoughts most of the time?" The answer may be a revelation.

One key distinction between success-oriented individuals and those who merely settle for mediocrity is their mindset, not just their actions. It's not uncommon for some people to read books and attend seminars on achieving success, yet they never seem to attain it. They may be doing all the "right" things, but it doesn't yield the same results as it does for others. The difference lies in their mindset and what truly matters.

In my experience advising individuals striving for uncharted territories, I've observed two distinct approaches. Some individuals discover their vision, prepare for it, and pursue it with unwavering confidence—they believe success is inevitable, and they succeed without hesitation. There's no doubt, no fear; they simply excel in what they do.

On the other hand, there are those who possess enthusiasm for their future but approach it with doubt, saying, "I hope this works out; things never seem to go my way." These individuals are destined to fail. Why? Because they've chosen to collapse before they even begin. They have nothing to gain because they've invested nothing. When they fail, they simply say, "I knew this would happen," and indeed, they expected it to happen.

Self-confidence is the belief that you will achieve what you set out to do.

It's not about being cocky or overconfident, thinking it will be a walk in the park. You're fully aware that it will require effort, that it won't be easy, but you're determined to succeed and will persevere until you do. As Henry Ford once said, "Whether you think you can or think you can't, you're right."

Any study of success will reveal that your mindset is the foremost and most critical aspect to get in order. If you harbor thoughts of failure, you're unlikely to accomplish what you set out to do. Success begins by saturating your mind with what you want to achieve, how you can achieve it, and what you must learn to move closer to your goal. As Earl Nightingale put it, "We become what we think about." Thought is a deliberate act; you must choose your thoughts and then work on maintaining them. The mind, left unchecked, tends to gravitate towards the negative. It's our instinct to consider the worst and let fear dominate our emotions. Successful individuals strive to maintain positive thoughts and focus on the task at hand. The human mind is a potent force, but it is effective only for those who work diligently to use it for the better, managing their emotions to achieve their goals.

We must always remember that the Creator has granted us control over just one aspect in the vast universe—ourselves and our emotions. We have no power over space, climate, or others. You and your emotions are the sole domain where you have control. Self-confidence empowers us to take charge of ourselves, becoming masters of our emotions rather than their captives.

"Confidence on the outside begins by living with integrity on the inside." - Brian Tracy

I once had a young man come to me for guidance many years ago.

Throughout his career and personal life, he faced a significant challenge and often felt as if he were trapped in a cave. When we sat down to talk, his initial statement to me was, "The last thing I want to hear about is that positive thinking nonsense." I told him that with that mindset, he had revealed why he was struggling so much and why he would continue to face difficulties in life. Believing that I shouldn't invest my time if there was no willingness to change, I suggested he seek guidance elsewhere.

Few things are as detrimental to success as a negative attitude. Negativity erodes our self-confidence and convinces us that we cannot achieve success.

Those who cling to a negative mindset understand all too well that progress eludes them, and they fail to reach the levels of success they aspire to. With what Zig Ziglar aptly termed "stinkin-thinkin," victory remains elusive.

A positive attitude, on the other hand, exponentially nurtures and strengthens self-confidence. You recognize that progress is possible when you feel good about yourself, your family, and your work environment. You form positive relationships with others, a key to success. People are more inclined to support and provide opportunities to those they like, while avoiding those with a less friendly disposition. Imagine having an open job position with two applicants: one highly skilled but with a negative attitude, and the other less experienced but with a positive attitude. Who would you choose? The positive attitude candidate, every time.

Successful individuals with positive attitudes believe they can achieve the seemingly impossible. They don't shy away from challenges; in fact, they find them exciting and enjoyable. They seek solutions instead of dwelling on obstacles. I concur with American author Theodore Roethke when he said, "What we need are more people who specialize in the impossible." A positive attitude not only makes you pleasant to be around but also uplifts your own spirits, leading to increased productivity and happiness. Positive people tend to become better, happier, and accomplish more. When you view each day as a gift and use it for good, you appreciate the blessings in your life. Positivity fosters the confidence needed to pursue even the most challenging dreams.

"The difference between a successful person and a loser is often not that one has superior talents or strategies, but the confidence to gamble on one's thoughts, take a calculated risk—and act." — Andre Malraux

Wise quotes hold immense power. As English poet Isaac D'Israeli stated, "Quotations embody the wisdom of the learned and the memory of ages." Quotes can serve as potent builders of self-confidence. They're like receiving a pep talk from Benjamin Franklin, Abraham Lincoln, Napoleon Hill, and many other luminaries throughout history. Here's a daily exercise that can help bolster your self-confidence and outlook on life: gather three meaningful quotes each day. These are words that resonate with you and provide encouragement. They're not hard to find; they abound on social media.

Try it for a week, and observe whether it makes a difference in your thinking and behavior.

However, here's the caveat: quotes alone won't make much of a difference if you don't genuinely believe in them. Let's examine some simple yet profound quotes, each expressing a fundamental truth that can transform your life if embraced and internalized.

"What the imagination can conceive or believe, it can achieve." - Napoleon Hill

"You are born to succeed, and the roots of success are within you." - Zig Ziglar

"Be assured that He who began a good work in you will carry it to completion." - St. Paul

I'm sure you've encountered these quotes numerous times and may even have them written down to revisit periodically. So, ask yourself this: "If you truly embraced these statements, how would your life be different?" You see, many of us say all the right words and have acquired valuable advice, but not many truly believe it as a reality.

Believing that you can succeed in life is the essence of self-confidence. It's not a mere attempt to win. It's not conditional on everything going perfectly. It's not contingent on receiving the support you desire. It's the unshakable belief that you will succeed. You may not know exactly how or when, but you know you will.

I'm certain you've heard or been asked the simple question, "What would you do if you knew you couldn't fail?" It goes beyond stimulating your imagination or motivating your actions; it's a genuine and profoundly important question. Your ability to answer this question will determine the fulfillment of your life.

How would you behave if you knew you couldn't fail? What aspirations would you pursue if you knew you couldn't fail? How would you feel throughout the day if you knew you couldn't fail? How would you interact with others if you knew you couldn't fail? What would your life be like when you KNOW you can't fail?

Here's why this question is so crucial. When you believe you can't fail to achieve that goal, you will carry yourself with confidence. You'll attempt things you might have considered improbable, now realizing they are not unthinkable. It's akin to the former United States Marine Corps motto: "We're doing the difficult right now; the impossible may take a little longer." This is a profound truth. Take a moment to prepare for it. Breathe slowly and sit up straight. Say it aloud then. "I can accept it as truth because I can't fail." Got it? Write it down once more, this time with unwavering certainty. Believe it; it's a reality. Those who genuinely believe they can't fail find success every time. Why? Because they never give up trying, believing they can't lose. They keep learning and progressing, motivated daily by the belief that they're drawing closer to their life goals. Trying to stop a speeding train with your bare hands is easier than halting someone who believes their dreams will be realized.

This is where faith becomes a fundamental aspect of the mindset of successful individuals. Speaking as a person of faith, I believe I was created for a purpose. God didn't randomly create me, and I'm not merely a statistical occurrence. It was God's intention that I exist at this moment to fulfill a part of His grand plan for all of life. So, if I was intentionally created by the Creator of the universe, do you not think He has every intention of ensuring I fulfill that purpose? I know it because I have faith that nothing can stand against me if God is for me. Be a person of faith and strive to be that. Know and believe that, as a successful person, you will achieve your dreams. What are the characteristics of a successful person? They are unmistakably these: they give their best effort, they have faith in God, they seek the unseen, and they transform their world.

Self-confidence emerges from within. However, some sources suggest that you can build self-confidence from the outside in, such as by acquiring a skill, achieving a goal, dressing well, or improving your physical appearance. While these approaches can certainly boost your self-confidence, they may not address the root cause of low self-confidence.

Because self-confidence originates from within, you must delve within to access it. Many self-help books suggest searching outside yourself to boost self-confidence, but looking outward can create a void that prevents you from truly understanding what's happening inside you. It won't help you discover the underlying causes of your low self-confidence. This approach doesn't build self-confidence on a solid foundation.

Genuine self-confidence is rooted in belief and mindset. You may excel in certain areas yet lack self-confidence, while you might encounter individuals who aren't particularly skilled in a specific field but exude self-assuredness.

This suggests that self-confidence may have little to do with achievements, skills, or outward presentation. What truly matters is your inner self-confidence.

Creating self-confidence is closely tied to our belief in ourselves and our goals. Throughout life, we encounter various challenges, starting from early childhood and growing in complexity as we mature. How we handle these challenges, particularly as adults, can greatly influence our success or lack thereof in various aspects of life and our careers.

Our self-confidence plays a significant role in shaping our future. When our self-confidence is high, our trust in our abilities grows, and conversely, when our self-confidence wanes, so does our trust.

Consider successful individuals, such as athletes, who face formidable odds in some situations, enduring repeated losses, yet maintain unwavering self-confidence and a "never say die" mentality. They refuse to surrender and see defeat as just another step on the path to success. Similarly, people with disabilities often exhibit incredible inner strength and self-confidence, achieving near-impossible feats.

In these examples, self-confidence is not optional; it is abundant and unwavering. Such deep and unwavering self-confidence keeps their self-esteem consistently high.

We, too, can cultivate this self-belief by possessing ambition, patience, and unwavering focus. Without these attributes, the goal of building self-confidence and making it a reality will remain unattainable.

Are you ready to start believing in yourself? What is your purpose? What will you do? Are you prepared to make a difference in your life? These are questions you must ask yourself to elevate your self-confidence to new heights.

Leave the past behind and embark on a new beginning. Believe that you are capable of achieving anything you set your mind to. Define your goals and don't give up until you achieve them. Nurture your faith and turn it into reality. It all begins within your mind, within those five inches!

Don't let setbacks overwhelm you. We all face setbacks; they are a part of life. How you handle them is what truly matters. View failure as a step closer to success. If Thomas Edison had given up, there would be no light bulbs. He persisted and succeeded!

Set your sights on the finish line and trust that your goals will be realized. With self-belief, there's something almost magical. You feel in control of everything you do, without doubt, or hesitation, and you have the courage to take the next step in all your endeavors.

Lack of self-belief often leads to indecision, and opportunities are missed because of anxiety. This stems from a lack of self-confidence.

Remember, your mind can hold only one thought at a time, so cling to the feeling of self-belief, that anything is possible, and don't allow negative thoughts to take its place.

Think about what you want to achieve every morning when you wake up. Treat setbacks as learning opportunities and keep moving forward in your daily pursuits. It's a journey, and you need to keep stepping up.

Before going to bed at the end of each day, take a moment to reflect on what you've accomplished. Be proud of the fact that you possess the attributes of inner self-belief, enabling you to think this way. When you start believing in yourself, you not only build confidence within yourself but also inspire others to believe in you.

Now, let's explore what you can do to enhance your inner self-confidence.

Embrace Failure as a Learning Experience

Change your perspective on failure. Do you become disheartened when faced with disappointment? Do you feel hopeless when things don't go as planned? At some point in life, we've all experienced this. It's because we tend to view failure as a loss.

For example, I had a major setback in my laboratory work in 2008. After five years of training, I couldn't believe how I had messed up the experiment. It felt like a colossal failure to me. I locked myself in my room for two days. However, from that experience, I gained valuable insights, picked myself up, and resumed my training.

Shift away from the notion that "loss equals failure." We've been conditioned to think that way, just like fearing a bad test score. This mindset has eroded our self-confidence.

Now, consider successful individuals today. How many of them have faced multiple setbacks? Quite a few. Despite facing numerous challenges, they persisted, learned, and emerged stronger.

Failure is not a defeat; it's merely a signal that something isn't working. With this new perspective, your life won't crumble; it will only offer suggestions and lessons. Nothing holds you back in that scenario; you can soar like an eagle. Simply changing this one belief can help you build self-confidence.

Live Life to the Fullest

Life is meant to be an adventure, filled with new experiences. When you begin to believe that you are here to truly experience life, you'll gain confidence and courage to venture into uncharted territories or tackle things you've always been afraid of.

Approach interactions with strangers as an opportunity to have a conversation with another human being and a chance for a new experience. Regardless of whether the conversation goes exceptionally well or not, it's a new experience for you.

In this mindset, the end result becomes less significant because it's about the experience itself. Life is about experiencing and learning. By embracing this approach, you can cultivate self-confidence through the process of gaining new experiences. You'll discover that self-confidence breeds more confidence in yourself. Ultimately, you'll find that you are already within your self-confidence. You achieve this by shifting from results-oriented thinking to experiential thinking.

Removing the Influence of Others

Lack of self-confidence often stems from concerns about how others perceive us. By shedding this anxiety, you can take significant steps toward boosting your self-confidence.

Frequently, our hesitation to pursue our desires is rooted in the fear of others' judgments. Many people refrain from singing loudly or expressing themselves fully because they worry about how others will perceive them. I've been in that position myself.

The day I decided to cast aside that insecurity and dance freely, regardless of how I looked, I realized that people generally don't pay as much attention to us as we think. Most strangers are preoccupied with their own lives and concerns, so they don't dwell on our actions.

Remember, how others perceive you is not about you—it's about their perception. If some people think your singing is terrible, it doesn't define your worth. You are being true to yourself, and you don't need to adopt their narrative.

When you choose to trust in yourself rather than being preoccupied with how others see you, your self-confidence is likely to flourish.

The goal here is to cultivate inner self-confidence. It has always resided within you; it's a part of who you are. Instead of trying to establish self-confidence, think of it as rediscovering and embracing the self-confidence that has always been there.

By practicing the three methods mentioned earlier and changing your unsupportive beliefs, you can witness a remarkable increase in your self-confidence.

Why Developing Self-Confidence Is Crucial for Self-Esteem Too

Self-confidence is an internal sense of complete trust and belief in oneself.

Successful individuals understand that they must first have confidence in their own ability to succeed. It starts with our mindset and then manifests in our actions.

It's the mentality of self-assurance—believing in what we say and what we can do. Hence, it's no surprise that self-confidence plays a crucial role in being effective in any area of our lives.

It's a state of mind, an attitude that shapes our behavior, and this attitude can be cultivated consciously. We can learn to have self-confidence by intentionally nurturing these attitudes.

Self-confidence is also closely linked to our self-worth.

Self-worth is a personal evaluation of one's own value and significance as an individual, in relation to others. It's difficult to manifest a sense of self-confidence without a reasonable level of self-worth.

Having a healthy sense of self-esteem is a significant factor in building robust self-confidence, and vice versa. By learning how to foster positivity and elevating the value we place on ourselves, we can greatly enrich our lives.

There's an element of bravery in our journey to becoming sure of our own abilities. Courage assists us in building self-confidence in the face of our anxieties.

A lack of self-confidence is often rooted in an irrational fear, particularly fear of the unknown. Such anxieties are closely tied to the fear of failure, embarrassment, rejection, ridicule, and the like, which are typically unfounded once the events have concluded.

When these groundless fears go unaddressed and unresolved, they can impede and hinder our ability to function effectively and successfully.

We all possess a certain degree of self-confidence, and this belief in ourselves can fluctuate over time and in different areas of our lives. It hinges on the daily challenges we face and our capacity to tackle them. Self-confidence may manifest in some areas but be lacking in others.

However, it's crucial to avoid confusing self-assuredness and a healthy sense of self-worth with arrogance. Arrogant individuals often lack self-confidence and use arrogance as a compensatory mechanism.

In truth, people with genuine self-confidence are humble enough to acknowledge that they are not always right. They are open to others' perspectives and do not take offense when their thoughts or beliefs are questioned. They engage in constructive dialogue and are willing to disagree amicably.

Individuals with self-confidence embrace lively discussions and are open to disagreement. Striving for a balanced and healthy sense of self-confidence should be our aim.

Building a stable and positive self-confidence is attainable.

The desired outcome of our deliberate action plan should be the enhancement of our self-confidence. It's essential to recognize from the outset that the reason we may lack trust in our own abilities is often a conscious choice we make.

I concur, it's about breaking free from the self-imposed belief that we can't excel! Right from the start, we must escape this psychological trap; for what we believe, we will achieve!

This simple yet profoundly emotionally satisfying act will uplift our spirits and enable us to have greater faith in ourselves. As we start to practice what we believe and embark on the journey of building self-confidence, we will generate more successes in our lives.

These accomplishments will, in turn, fuel our confidence-building efforts. As our self-confidence is reinforced by the positive outcomes and triumphs we consistently achieve, our self-worth will also increase, enhancing our sense of personal value.

This is a method for learning how to build self-confidence. Challenges will not deter those who are genuinely committed to enhancing their self-confidence; instead, they will be motivated by them.

Just like we systematically and intentionally build our muscles, we also build our self-confidence. With each minor achievement, we gain a higher level of enhanced self-confidence.

Every success contributes to the construction of self-confidence.

Ultimately, we will learn to rely on ourselves and our own judgments without hesitation or fear.

Here are some exercises and strategies to develop self-confidence:

1. **Start creating a journal:** Begin a journal to conduct a self-analysis. Identify your self-confidence ideas and write down your thoughts. Reflect on what may be holding you back from achieving your goals.

2. **Recharge:** Take time for emotional, physical, and spiritual rejuvenation. Find moments of peace and solitude to recharge.

3. **Carry out a self-assessment:** Objectively assess yourself without relying on the opinions of others. Focus on your thoughts, feelings, behavior, and lifestyle to gain self-awareness.

4. **Recognize and respect yourself:** Embrace and respect your uniqueness. Acknowledge your strengths and qualities, and avoid comparing yourself to others.

5. **Focus on your strengths:** Concentrate on your abilities and positive qualities. Recognize your strengths and celebrate your achievements, no matter how small they may seem.

6. **Conquer challenges and fears:** Don't let fear of failure hold you back. Embrace challenges and approach them with confidence, knowing that failures are opportunities for growth.

7. **Inspire yourself:** Encourage yourself daily by acknowledging your accomplishments. Keep a list of tasks you've done well to boost your self-confidence.

8. **Engage in positive self-talk:** Replace negative thoughts with positive affirmations. Challenge pessimism with thoughts of positivity and success.

9. **Visualize your future success:** Imagine yourself succeeding in your endeavors. Feel the excitement, joy, and confidence that come with success.

10. **Acknowledge your achievements:** Give yourself credit for your accomplishments, no matter how small. Reward yourself and reflect on past successes to build confidence.

11. **Accept failure and reframe:** Learn from your mistakes and view them as opportunities for growth. Don't dwell on past failures; instead, focus on improvement.

12. **Take risks:** Step out of your comfort zone and embrace new challenges.

Don't fear making mistakes, as they are part of the learning process.

13. **Behave with confidence:** Project confidence in your actions and demeanor. Believe in your capabilities and maintain a positive self-image.

14. **Attend seminars:** Participate in seminars with knowledgeable and motivating speakers who offer guidance on building self-confidence. Observe their speaking styles and learn from their confidence.

These exercises and strategies can help you develop and maintain self-confidence in various aspects of your life. Use them to work towards a more confident and empowered self.

Initiating the process of building self-confidence is crucial for personal growth and success. Whether it's breaking free from negative self-doubt or reinforcing positive beliefs, here's how you can kickstart this transformation:

1. Recognize the Snowball Effect: Understand that self-confidence can either grow positively or negatively, depending on your experiences and mindset. This awareness is the first step in taking control.

2. Start with Small Steps: Begin by taking small, manageable steps in areas where you want to boost your confidence. Success in these smaller tasks can lay the foundation for more significant achievements.

3. Embrace Failure: Accept that failure is a part of the process. When you encounter setbacks, view them as opportunities to learn and improve, rather than as reasons to give up.

4. Challenge Negative Beliefs: Identify and challenge self-imposed limitations and negative beliefs that have hindered your confidence. Replace them with positive affirmations and constructive thoughts.

5. Seek Positive Influences: Surround yourself with supportive and encouraging people who believe in your capabilities. Positive influences can help you break free from self-doubt.

6. Create a Positive Feedback Loop: Whenever you succeed, no matter how small the achievement, acknowledge and celebrate it. This positive reinforcement will reinforce your self-confidence.

7. Focus on Self-Improvement: Continuously work on improving your skills and knowledge in areas that matter to you. The more you invest in self-improvement, the more confident you'll become.

8. Visualize Success: Practice visualizing yourself succeeding in your goals. Imagine the feelings of accomplishment and confidence that come with achieving your objectives.

9. Challenge Negative Conditioning: Recognize that many self-imposed limitations are a result of societal conditioning. Challenge these beliefs and prove them wrong through your actions.

10. Learn from Role Models: Study the lives of individuals who have overcome adversity and achieved greatness despite facing criticism or doubt. Their stories can inspire and motivate you.

11. Cultivate Resilience: Develop resilience to bounce back from failures and setbacks. Understand that temporary setbacks don't define your overall potential.

12. Seek Professional Help: If deep-seated self-doubt or confidence issues are holding you back, consider seeking the assistance of a therapist or counselor to work through these issues.

Building self-confidence is a gradual process that requires patience and persistence. By taking these steps and understanding the power of the positive and negative "snowball effect," you can initiate a transformative journey toward greater self-confidence and personal success.

Reversing negative self-confidence is not only possible but also achievable through various strategies aimed at reshaping your thought patterns and building self-esteem. Here's how you can begin to transform your self-confidence:

1. Challenge Negative Thoughts: Start by recognizing and challenging negative thought patterns that have eroded your self-confidence. Replace them with positive and constructive thoughts.

2. Positive Affirmations: Use positive affirmations to reprogram your mind. These are uplifting statements that you repeat to yourself to create new patterns of thought. Embrace them with conviction and emotion to reinforce self-confidence.

3. Guided Visualization: Engage in guided visualization exercises where you mentally picture yourself achieving success and feeling confident. This helps create a positive image in your mind.

4. Cognitive Imagery: Practice cognitive imagery by visualizing successful outcomes and situations in which you exude confidence. This mental rehearsal can boost your self-assurance.

5. Goal-Oriented Training: Set clear and achievable goals for yourself. Accomplishing these goals, no matter how small, can significantly boost your confidence.

6. Breathing Strategies: Learn and practice deep breathing techniques to reduce anxiety and stress, which can contribute to low self-confidence.

7. Subliminal Software: Consider using subliminal software or recordings designed to promote positive thinking and confidence-building.

8. Whole-Brain Practice: Engage in activities that stimulate both hemispheres of your brain, fostering creativity and enhancing your problem-solving abilities, which can contribute to self-confidence.

To get you started, here are some test affirmations you can use to build self-confidence:

- I liberate myself from artificial constraints and choose to be self-confident.
- I radiate self-confidence and feel confident in my abilities.
- I resist cynicism at all levels of consciousness.
- I transform pessimism into optimism.
- The more productive I become, the more confident I feel.
- I am a positive person who exudes self-confidence.
- I am smart, competent, and capable.

Use these affirmations regularly, repeating them with conviction and emotion. You can also practice them while looking in the mirror to reinforce your self-esteem and project confidence to others. As you consistently apply these strategies, you'll begin to notice a positive shift in your self-confidence, setting you on a path toward greater self-assurance and success.

To initiate the process of building self-confidence, it's crucial to recognize that consistency and positive emotions are key. While there are numerous methods to develop self-confidence and self-esteem, it's important to commit to a plan that works for you. Some people find that audio programs are an effective way to maintain continuity and develop positive thinking patterns. These programs often include a range of techniques such as positive affirmations, guided visualizations, cognitive mapping, goal-oriented relaxation, subliminal processing, and more.

Regardless of the method you choose, the essential thing is to remain dedicated to enhancing your self-confidence. Seek support from friends, family, or a therapist if necessary, as it's too important to let go of. Rest assured that your confidence can be strengthened, and it has the power to positively transform your life.

Self-confidence is a priceless quality that influences every aspect of our lives. Without it, we can't function effectively or pursue our goals. Brian Tracy emphasizes the importance of self-confidence in his self-confidence program, "The Science of Self-Confidence." Whether you believe you can or can't, you're right. Your beliefs and self-confidence are what drive your actions and determine your outcomes.

Certainty is a fundamental human need, and when we lack confidence, we become paralyzed by uncertainty. However, self-confidence isn't something you're born with; it's a mindset that can be cultivated and practiced. You can deliberately develop habits that make you more optimistic and self-assured. It's a systematic process, much like building physical muscles, and it can either support you or hold you back. The cycle of self-confidence is self-reinforcing: the more you act confidently, the more confidence you build, making it easier to continue doing so.

Investing in a reputable self-confidence program can be invaluable. Building self-confidence is not an easy task, and self-confident individuals have mastered the ability to activate their self-confidence in various areas of their lives, even when they haven't achieved prior success or when they're feeling fearful. Developing self-confidence is a science, not a quick fix or magic solution. It's about changing your self-perception, and this is a vital element in improving self-confidence.

Your ability to pursue and achieve your goals is closely tied to your level of self-confidence. To be truly successful in whatever you aspire to be, do, or have in life, you must have confidence in yourself. Trustworthy people exude confidence, making them attractive in more ways than one. Self-confidence is the key to unlocking your potential and taking control of your life.

Hypnosis for self-confidence is a highly effective method for boosting self-esteem and reclaiming a sense of self-worth.

Low self-esteem can lead to various vulnerabilities and anxieties that can be challenging to overcome. Often, these feelings have deep roots in your past and can become increasingly difficult to manage over time. Despite your efforts to maintain a positive attitude and remind yourself of your many positive qualities, you may find yourself struggling to maintain positive energy and self-confidence.

If you've been trying to combat low self-esteem and feel frustrated by your efforts, don't give up hope. Hypnosis for self-confidence can offer a way out of this negative mindset by interacting with your mind at a deeper level, where fears, phobias, and other negative influences have been stored since early in your life.

Hypnosis is a powerful tool for addressing internal challenges. Some people still have misconceptions about hypnotherapy, fearing that they will lose control of their actions and be vulnerable to manipulation. In reality, during hypnosis, you are in a state of deep mental relaxation and heightened suggestibility, but you remain in control and aware of your surroundings.

Hypnosis was first introduced by James Braid, a Scottish physician, in the late 1800s. The terms "hypnosis" and "hypnotism" essentially mean "nervous system rest," as it brings individuals to a state of deep mental relaxation. In this state, the mind becomes more accessible and receptive to positive suggestions, freeing it from constant negative self-talk.

Hypnosis for self-confidence involves guiding individuals to a state of mental tranquility through verbal instructions. In this state, a therapist or individual, often using a recorded voice or a guided self-hypnosis mp3 or CD, can work through positive visualizations and constructive feedback to help individuals achieve their self-confidence goals. It allows you to see yourself in a new light, free from worries, apprehensions, mistakes, or concerns about others.

Through hypnosis for self-confidence, you and the therapist (or the audio-guided self-hypnosis) can focus on bringing out your inner beauty, ideal self, and a sense of worthiness. By creating new positive self-confidence and removing external influences, you can experience a transformation in how you perceive your abilities and self-worth. You'll be pleasantly surprised when you next contemplate your skills and potential.

Chapter 4: The Relationship Between Self-Confidence and Forgiveness

When it comes to self-confidence, forgiveness plays a significant role. It's essential to remind ourselves who we need to forgive when we struggle with self-confidence. Forgiveness is the key to breaking free from the chains that hold us back, liberating us from our emotional prisons.

Holding onto past hurts ties us to the person or event that harmed us through an emotional bond. The only way to sever this connection is through forgiveness.

Forgiveness is a gift we give ourselves for our own higher good. It means we no longer define our lives by the extent of our pain but by the extent of our growth. Forgiving doesn't mean we're letting others off the hook scot-free; it means we're releasing ourselves from the burden of resentment. We can move forward with unwavering confidence, unburdened by our past.

Clutching onto grudges for too long only deepens our sense of injustice and keeps us stuck. We might still remember the person who hurt us for what they were, even though they may have evolved into a much better person than before.

With forgiveness comes a fresh perspective, enabling us to rebuild our lives. When we genuinely forgive someone, we can begin to accept what happened to us and understand things from their point of view. We realize the inner struggle they might have endured, which can be incredibly empowering.

This means that as we navigate our lives, we can choose to embrace any painful experiences we encounter. We won't hold onto them by sacrificing others in the process, nor will we relinquish our strength. No one should ever have the power to strip us of our strength.

Once we've forgiven others for past hurts, we can start to restore our faith and self-esteem. We can adopt new, stronger beliefs that propel us from a state of stagnation to a position of self-empowerment. This inner strength allows us to live the life we were meant to live.

The cycle of forgiveness has two aspects: forgiving others for what they have done or what we believed they did to us, and forgiving ourselves for harboring negative feelings about them and allowing their influence over us.

Say yes to forgiveness and release yourself from the past. The power lies in the present moment. You have the ability to create a life for yourself.

High self-esteem and self-confidence can have a profound impact on your life, attracting better things and experiences. Here's how:

1. **Improved Professional Life**: When you have high self-confidence, you're more likely to speak up at work, ask for help when needed, and pursue career advancement opportunities. This can lead to increased job satisfaction, better pay, and more success in your professional life.

2. **Healthy Relationships**: High self-esteem and self-confidence are essential for healthy relationships. You'll feel secure in your partnerships, knowing that you are valued for who you are. This confidence allows you to communicate openly, handle difficult conversations, and maintain strong, fulfilling connections.

3. **Emotional Well-Being**: With increased self-confidence, you wake up each day feeling positive and energized, ready to tackle the day's challenges. While everyone has their share of ordinary days, you can navigate them without spiraling into extended periods of negativity or self-doubt.

4. **Stress Reduction**: Confidence helps you handle stressful situations more effectively. You're less likely to be overwhelmed by daily stressors, and you can approach problems with a calm and collected mindset, finding solutions rather than dwelling on the issues.

5. **Social Connections**: Confidence makes it easier to fit in with social groups and make new friends. You're more likely to engage in social activities and expand your network, leading to richer social experiences and opportunities.

6. **Personal Growth**: Building self-confidence and self-esteem is an ongoing process, but the more you invest in it, the more you'll grow as an individual. You'll become more resilient, adaptable, and open to new experiences.

7. **Relationship Satisfaction**: In a healthy partnership, both individuals feel secure and valued. When you have high self-esteem, you can contribute positively to your relationship, fostering trust, communication, and mutual respect.

8. **Effective Communication**: Confidence allows you to express yourself clearly and assertively. You can address difficult topics without fear of conflict, ensuring that your needs and boundaries are respected.

9. **Reduced Anxiety**: With self-confidence, you're less likely to dwell on negative thoughts and anxieties. You can manage your emotions better and approach life's challenges with a more positive outlook.

10. **Resilience**: Confidence helps you bounce back from setbacks and failures. You view challenges as opportunities for growth rather than insurmountable obstacles.

While building self-confidence and self-esteem may take time and effort, the benefits are well worth it. These qualities empower you to lead a more fulfilling and rewarding life, attracting positivity and success along the way.

Absolutely, high self-confidence can have a significant impact on various aspects of your life, leading to numerous benefits and positive experiences:

1. **Improved Relationships**: Confidence makes it easier to meet new people and form healthy, fulfilling relationships. Others are often drawn to self-confident individuals because they exude positivity and assurance.

2. **Healthy Partnerships**: When you have confidence in yourself, you're more likely to enter into relationships for the right reasons rather than seeking external validation. This can lead to more meaningful and long-lasting partnerships.

3. **Quality Social Life**: Confidence enables you to enjoy social events and activities with ease. You feel respected and valued in your social circles, fostering a vibrant and enjoyable social life.

4. **Enhanced Time Management**: Self-confidence can help you stay organized and focused, allowing you to handle challenges efficiently and create a balanced work-life schedule. This, in turn, provides more quality time for your loved ones and personal pursuits.

5. **Professional Success**: Confidence at work can boost your productivity, efficiency, and ability to connect with colleagues and superiors. It can

lead to career advancement and the pursuit of your dream job.

6. **Emotional Resilience**: High self-confidence equips you to deal with life's challenges, setbacks, and losses with greater resilience. You recognize that your self-worth is not tied to external events or others' opinions, giving you a sense of control over your life.

7. **Stress Management**: Confident individuals are better equipped to handle stress and remain composed in difficult situations. This can lead to reduced stress levels and an overall sense of calm.

8. **Sense of Fulfillment**: Confidence can boost your sense of self-worth and achievement, both personally and professionally. You can pursue your goals with determination, knowing you have the ability to succeed.

9. **Inner Strength**: Self-confidence helps you cultivate inner strength and self-reliance. You become less dependent on external validation and more focused on your own growth and happiness.

10. **Positive Outlook**: Confidence fosters a positive mindset, allowing you to approach life with optimism and a belief in your capabilities. This positivity can attract more positive experiences into your life.

In summary, high self-confidence can be a transformative force, leading to better relationships, a fulfilling social life, professional success, and improved overall well-being. It provides the inner strength and resilience to navigate life's challenges with grace and optimism.

Absolutely, the relationship between assertiveness and self-confidence is closely intertwined. Assertiveness is a key component of self-confidence, and developing assertiveness can significantly enhance one's overall confidence. Here's a closer look at how assertiveness and self-confidence are connected and some tips on becoming more assertive and confident:

1. **Assertiveness and Self-Confidence**: Assertiveness involves standing up for your rights and expressing your thoughts, feelings, and needs in a respectful and confident manner. When you are assertive, you demonstrate self-assurance and belief in your own worth, which is a fundamental aspect of self-confidence.

2. **Positive Body Language**: Assertive communication is often accompanied by positive body language, such as maintaining good posture, keeping an open stance (no crossed arms), and making direct eye contact. This body language not only conveys confidence to others but also reinforces your self-confidence.

3. **Using "I" Statements**: Assertiveness involves using "I" statements to express your thoughts and feelings assertively. By saying phrases like "I feel," "I think," or "I believe," you take ownership of your perspective, which can boost your self-confidence by reinforcing your right to express yourself.

4. **Setting Boundaries**: Assertive individuals set and maintain healthy boundaries, which is essential for self-confidence. When you establish boundaries and communicate them assertively, you protect your self-esteem and demonstrate self-respect.

5. **Self-Belief and Action**: The more you practice assertiveness and experience positive outcomes, the more your subconscious mind starts to believe in your ability to assert yourself effectively. This self-belief can translate into greater self-confidence in various areas of life.

6. **Overcoming Fear**: Becoming assertive often involves overcoming the fear of conflict or rejection. As you face and conquer these fears through assertive behavior, your self-confidence grows because you learn that you can handle challenging situations with grace and composure.

7. **Continuous Improvement**: Like self-confidence, assertiveness is a skill that can be developed over time. It's important to recognize that both are ongoing journeys. You can always strive to improve your assertiveness skills, which, in turn, will continue to bolster your self-confidence.

In summary, assertiveness and self-confidence go hand in hand. Becoming more assertive not only helps you express yourself effectively but also reinforces your belief in your own capabilities, ultimately leading to greater self-confidence. It's a valuable skill to cultivate for personal and professional growth.

CHAPTER 5: The Significance of Self-Confidence in Sports

Self-confidence is a vital attribute not only for successful business people, authors, managers, rulers, and presidents but also for athletes. In fact, self-confidence plays a crucial role in both personal and sports success.

If you ask any accomplished sports coach, they will tell you that an athlete's self-confidence can be the deciding factor between victory and defeat, greatness and mediocrity. Consider this scenario: two teams with excellent players, sound tactical strategies, and top-notch physical fitness, all motivated by the prospect of a financial reward. However, if even one player on either team lacks self-confidence and doubts their abilities, that team's chances of winning decrease significantly.

While external motivation, like financial rewards, can be a factor, it's not enough on its own. What truly drives exceptional performance is often the internal motivation that stems from within the individual or the team. It could be the desire to excel, to make one's family or nation proud, or another deeply personal source of inspiration.

In sports, self-confidence is paramount. Whether it's a team sport or an individual endeavor, the belief that you can give your absolute best without fear of failure is a game-changer. Have you ever witnessed a talented athlete who performed poorly during a competition due to extreme nervousness? This is a prime example of lacking self-confidence. To succeed in sports, you must learn to remain calm, trust in your abilities, banish negative thoughts, and stay focused on your goals.

It's important to remember that making mistakes is a part of the game, and it's perfectly normal. The key is to acknowledge your mistakes, learn from them, and avoid comparing yourself to others. If someone else is performing better, it's alright; your primary focus should always be on your own objectives.

Self-Confidence in Teenagers: Building Resilience

The teenage years often resemble navigating a turbulent sea of emotions. Adolescents grapple with uncertainty, depression, and the challenging transition from childhood to adulthood. As their bodies undergo significant changes, feelings of guilt can surface. The pressure to fit in socially and adapt to the demands of school can weigh heavily on them. These challenges can erode a teenager's self-confidence, leaving them feeling vulnerable and powerless, which not only affects them but also concerns their family and friends. **Here are some strategies to help teenagers bolster their self-confidence during this tumultuous period:**

1. Understand Teenagers: It's crucial to recognize that teenagers may grapple with self-confidence issues, and it's important to intervene when necessary. Help them realize their worth at this stage of life. Offer compliments, such as praising their academic achievements or thanking them for their contributions to household chores or service clubs. Express how valuable their efforts are to you. This will instill a sense of self-worth in them.

2. Encourage Sports and Activities: Engaging in sports and other activities provides both mental and physical stimulation. Encourage your teenager to participate in a sport of their choice. You can even join them in a sports club and practice together. If sports aren't their preference, consider other activities that require dedication and effort, like music lessons. These pursuits not only provide focus but also teach patience and offer a sense of accomplishment.

3. Involve Them in Decision-Making: Acknowledge that your teenagers are growing up, and they will soon be young adults. Therefore, it's essential to nurture their decision-making skills, fostering independence and responsibility. While some parents may doubt their children's decision-making abilities, giving them opportunities to make choices can be eye-opening. By involving them in decisions, you empower them and help build their self-confidence.

4. Recognize Warning Signs: While your teenager may be on the cusp of adulthood, they still face challenges and dilemmas that they may not fully understand or know how to handle. They inadvertently emit signals when grappling with problems. Your role is to detect these signals and initiate discussions. By doing so, your teenager will realize they're not alone and can turn to you for support whenever needed.

These strategies can help teenagers navigate the tricky waters of adolescence and emerge with enhanced self-confidence and resilience.

Improving Self-Confidence: A Journey to Self-Discovery

One of life's most significant goals is to improve self-confidence. Nobody should spend their life despising who they are. Each one of us possesses something unique, regardless of our backgrounds or circumstances. It's up to us to uncover it. Once we do, we can draw upon this inner strength to bolster our self-confidence.

1. Get to Know Yourself:

Self-discovery is a pivotal step toward enhancing self-confidence. We spend our entire lives with ourselves, but how well do we truly know who we are? Take the time to explore your inner self. Write down your thoughts, ask yourself probing questions, and delve into your heart's desires.

Recording the events of your day can unveil patterns, revealing both positive and negative qualities and behaviors. By doing this, you position yourself in the arena to understand who you really are. No longer should you give undue importance to negative traits and behaviors. Treat both positive and negative aspects as equally valuable, working on improving what you'd like to change and further cultivating your strengths.

2. Identify and Develop Your Talents:

Every individual possesses a unique gift waiting to be discovered and nurtured. Identifying and developing your talents is paramount. Consider what you enjoy doing so much that you'd do it for free. It may sound cliché, but it's crucial. I discovered my passion for physical activity, particularly exercise, which helped me gain confidence.

I grew up without participating in sports or formal training, feeling rather worthless. However, as I entered my late teens and began playing football, I excelled. This realization boosted my self-confidence significantly.

3. Remove Negative Influences:

Surrounding yourself with negative people can undermine your efforts to improve self-confidence, no matter how much self-discovery and talent development you undertake. If you have individuals in your life who are consistently unkind or critical, it's crucial to distance yourself from them. If severing ties is challenging, consider spending less time with them. Protect yourself emotionally, mentally, and physically. Communicate tactfully about your journey to self-discovery and self-confidence, explaining that distancing yourself is part of that process.

4. Practice Self-Care:

Engage in daily self-care practices that nurture rather than harm you. Regular physical activity offers numerous benefits. If you dislike traditional exercise, explore other options like dancing, joining a team, or learning a new sport. Whatever you choose, ensure it brings you joy and allows you to expend energy while appreciating yourself.

Additionally, carve out time for non-destructive self-indulgence. Whether it's a daily run, meditation, painting, car maintenance, or simply enjoying a long, relaxing bath, make it a habit to do something for yourself each day. Discover activities you're passionate about and start falling in love with yourself along the way.

Setting and Achieving Goals for Lasting Confidence

In the pursuit of confidence, I've found that setting and achieving immediate goals is crucial. While I have various long-term and short-term ambitions, it's the immediate goals that boost my self-assurance on a daily basis. They provide me with tangible accomplishments that I can be proud of daily, proving to myself that I can overcome challenges.

Here are some examples of my immediate goals:

1. Wake up earlier than anyone else.
2. Push myself during workouts, giving my best effort.
3. Never give up, even when faced with the desire to quit.

Self-Confidence in Women

Recent studies have shed light on the issue of self-confidence, particularly among women, and have shown that females are more likely to struggle with low self-esteem. This problem seems to be particularly prevalent among intelligent women, who often underestimate their own abilities and qualities.

Low self-confidence in females can be a pervasive issue, leading to a range of related problems. Women are often more susceptible to criticism and external influence, which can result in frequent changes of opinion and lowered self-esteem. In contrast, boys tend to enjoy challenging tasks and display more self-confidence and determination.

Research conducted at Michigan University has identified several factors contributing to this situation. Girls receive less encouragement for independence compared to boys and often receive more parental protection. They also face less social pressure to establish their own identities.

As a result, girls may become more confined to their immediate environments and have limited opportunities for self-discovery. Their inability to cope effectively with the world due to these limitations can further erode their confidence. To maintain their relationships with adults, they may feel compelled to prioritize dependence over independence, further damaging their self-confidence.

To address this lack of self-confidence, individuals must consider some fundamental questions:

- Am I always required to seek the opinions of others after making a decision?
- Should I be concerned about what others will think when I make a particular judgment or take a specific action?
- What steps can I take to enhance my self-confidence when making decisions?

Answering these questions honestly and thoughtfully can be the first step toward regaining self-confidence. It's essential to recognize that change won't happen overnight; it's a gradual process that requires taking one step at a time. However, the key is taking ownership of one's life once again.

Here are some essential strategies for boosting women's self-confidence:

1. Engage in activities that genuinely interest and excite you. For instance, if you aspire to be a fashion designer, take design classes, attend fashion shows, create your own collections, and don't be overly concerned about the judgments of others. Embrace your unique style and set trends.

Creating a List of Your Achievements and Employees for Self-Confidence

To boost self-confidence, one effective strategy is to begin by creating a list of your accomplishments and acknowledging the individuals who work with you. Taking these steps can significantly alter the trajectory of your life and positively impact the lives of those around you.

Research indicates that women are more likely to grapple with low self-confidence compared to men, affecting their emotions, behavior, and thoughts. Building a strong sense of self-confidence across various aspects of life, such as friendships, work, and social situations, can lead to personal growth and progress.

Here are some valuable tips for improving women's self-confidence:

1. Define how you want others to perceive you and align your actions

accordingly. People often assume that those who appear confident are trustworthy and treat them accordingly. Evidence suggests that behaving confidently can lead to long-term increases in self-confidence, even if one doesn't initially feel completely comfortable in that role.

2. Be honest about your strengths and weaknesses. It's common to focus on areas where we may not excel, rather than considering our overall capabilities. Some people may evaluate their performance based on areas they feel they should be proficient in, even if those areas aren't their natural talents. For instance, a woman's self-confidence might suffer because she believes she should excel in a particular sport when her true strengths lie in more artistic pursuits. Recognizing and appreciating one's true strengths can boost confidence.

3. Success and positive responses can reinforce self-confidence. Women often excel at multitasking, but this can sometimes lead to frustration when they can't fully focus on a single task. Consider simplifying your workload when working on projects or managing a reasonable number of responsibilities simultaneously.

4. Avoid being influenced by unrealistic portrayals of women in the media. Modern media often presents distorted images of women, contributing to feelings of inadequacy regarding appearance and body shape. Instead, embrace your natural appearance and assets, appreciating what makes you unique.

5. A healthy sense of self-esteem and confidence can benefit various aspects of life and can be self-sustaining in terms of success and achievement. Begin the journey with small steps, focusing on one aspect at a time, as meaningful changes often take time to manifest.

Boosting the Self-Confidence of Children

When parents nurture a child's confidence, they impart a positive message that can resonate throughout their lives. The early years of how parents interact with their children can significantly influence their level of self-assurance later in life. Mothers who foster self-belief in their children equip them with the essential foundation needed to thrive in the world.

A child's self-confidence largely relies on how those who are significant to them perceive and treat them. Families that attend to their children's needs are constructing the framework and trust that fosters self-worth. Children will grow up knowing that someone genuinely cares about them in the world.

While children may encounter negative influences attempting to undermine their self-esteem, parents should actively work to bolster their children's confidence. Parents should continue to embrace and embrace their children, reminding them of their uniqueness. Families should be responsive to their children's challenges, whether they face difficulties at school or with friends, and strive to offer positive solutions to their problems. Parents need not always agree with their children, but they should lend an empathetic ear to their concerns, maintaining the same kindness and love that they displayed during their early years. Children are especially sensitive to how they are treated, and if parents cease expressing affection and concern, it can have a detrimental impact on a child's self-assurance. While growing up, children will encounter various challenges and transitions, but with their parents' support and love, these transitions will be smoother, and they will have confidence in making the right decisions in life.

Parents may sometimes have busy schedules, leaving them with limited time for their children. Such parents should recognize that any missed opportunities with their children can potentially hinder their growth. Families should understand that forming a strong bond and having fun with their children is a precious relationship that can never be broken. This can only happen if parents dedicate more time to their children. Children can discern when parents are genuinely interested in spending time with them, so parents should genuinely engage with their children.

Parents should take note of what educational interests are important to their child as they grow. If a child shows an interest in numerical games, parents may consider involving them in math-related activities. As the child enhances their math skills while having fun, their confidence is likely to soar. Children, like adults, take pride in excelling at something. As the child develops an interest in other areas of learning, parents should nurture that interest by enrolling them in programs that support their passion. The more proficient they become, the more secure they feel in those pursuits.

Parents sometimes forget that, just like adults, children are individuals with thoughts and concerns. It is essential to treat children with respect as if they were young adults. Parents should attentively listen when children express their opinions on various matters. This gives the child the impression that their input matters and is genuinely considered within the family. Trust is built in this process.

The words parents choose when communicating with their children are also of utmost importance. When addressing children, parents should aim to be encouraging and positive, refraining from using derogatory language. Constantly putting children down is one of the quickest ways to erode their self-confidence. Parents should always strive to uplift their children. Parents can rephrase their words to be more positive, such as describing a hyperactive child as curious or remarking on their interesting personality rather than labeling them as dumb. This subtle shift in a child's life can make a significant difference in their self-confidence.

Fostering Self-Confidence in Children: A Parent's Role

Parents play a crucial role in nurturing their children's self-confidence, which can have a profound impact on their future. How parents engage with their children during their formative years can significantly shape their level of self-assurance later in life. Mothers and fathers who help instill self-belief in their children equip them with the foundation they need to navigate the world successfully.

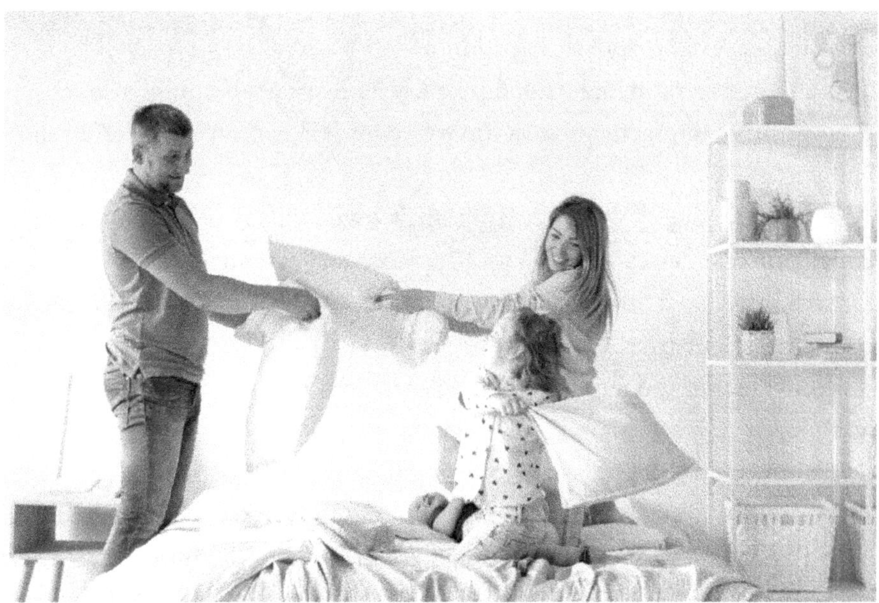

Children's self-confidence is largely influenced by how those who are important to them perceive and treat them. Families that attend to their children's needs are laying the groundwork for the trust and self-worth that fosters their natural curiosity. Children will grow up knowing that someone genuinely cares about them in the world.

As children grow and form friendships, they will encounter external influences, both positive and negative. Parents should take an active role in understanding their children's social circles and the kind of friends they associate with. This may occasionally lead to disagreements with their children, but it's essential to prioritize their well-being.

Participating in sports can be a powerful way to boost children's confidence. Even if children don't become superstar athletes, they gain valuable skills that contribute to emotional, psychological, and overall self-confidence. Recognizing and supporting a child's interests, whether in sports or other activities, is key.

Ultimately, parents who spend quality time with their children, engage with them emotionally, show affection, inspire them, encourage positive activities, listen attentively, and make their children feel valued contribute to raising happy and successful kids. Parents striving to be good role models can instill a strong sense of trust in their children.

As children grow in understanding, their increasing self-confidence reflects their positive interactions with the world and their growing belief in their abilities.

Self-confidence is about trusting one's own skills and having the inner conviction that one can make sound decisions and judgments. This self-belief is often reinforced through our interactions with others, further enhancing our sense of integrity.

Ideally, self-confidence is cultivated early in life and continues to develop as children gain experience and understanding.

Rapid, positive, and consistent nurturing, such as breastfeeding, provides infants with a foundation on which they build their sense of self-confidence.

The following strategies can help parents develop self-confidence in their children:

Avoid Making Comparisons: It's crucial not to compare children, especially within the family. Comparisons can lead to feelings of inadequacy and erode self-confidence. Each child is unique, and their individual qualities should be celebrated.

Acknowledge Their Abilities: Parents should refrain from underestimating their child's capabilities, even in simple tasks. Encouraging independence and letting them try things on their own can boost self-confidence. Instead of saying, "Let me do that for you," try saying, "Can you show me how you can do it?"

Promote Social Interaction: Encouraging regular social interaction with other children and their families can help develop self-confidence in social situations. Playing with peers and learning to communicate effectively fosters confidence in social settings.

Establish Boundaries: Setting consistent boundaries for a child helps create a sense of security and predictability, reducing anxiety-inducing situations.

Foster a Routine: Maintaining a regular and effective routine in daily life can instill confidence. Predictable daily activities provide a sense of structure and security.

Expose to New Experiences: Introducing a child to new places, people, and activities can broaden their horizons and build confidence. Encourage curiosity and exploration.

Open Communication: Encouraging children to express their feelings and emotions openly is essential. Teach them to use words to describe their emotions, fostering emotional intelligence and self-awareness.

Praise and Encourage: Celebrate your child's achievements and efforts regularly. Recognize their accomplishments, no matter how small, and let them know that their actions are appreciated.

Share Responsibilities: Assigning age-appropriate responsibilities to children allows them to feel capable and builds their sense of responsibility. As they grow, increase the complexity of their tasks.

Spend Quality Time: Playing and spending time with your child sends a powerful message of love and appreciation. Quality time strengthens the parent-child bond and boosts a child's self-esteem.

Encourage Acts of Confidence: Support and encourage your child to take on tasks that require self-confidence. Instead of doing things for them, guide and teach them to do it themselves.

Incorporating these strategies into parenting practices can help children develop self-confidence, fostering their overall well-being and growth.

Conclusion

In conclusion, life is unpredictable and often throws challenges our way. Whether it's in our careers, relationships, or personal well-being, our self-worth and self-confidence play a central role in how we navigate these challenges.

Self-confidence is like a thread that ties together the various aspects of our lives. It's the unwavering belief that even when things don't go as planned, we have the inner strength to face adversity and emerge stronger.

When life takes unexpected turns, it's easy to doubt ourselves and wonder if we'll ever find our way back to the light. However, it's important to remember that self-confidence isn't a fixed state; it's a dynamic evaluation of how we perceive ourselves, moment by moment.

Body image is one area where self-confidence often comes into play, and it can manifest differently in men and women. While both genders may have moments of body image insecurity, women, in particular, often face societal pressures to meet certain beauty standards. These pressures can influence their self-confidence and body image.

In a world where images of unrealistic beauty standards flood the internet, it's important to recognize that self-confidence is a universal concern. No one exists on a self-confidence "island." We all grapple with moments of self-doubt and the desire to fit in and be accepted.

When traditional self-help tips fall short in boosting self-confidence, seeking professional help like counseling, life coaching, or hypnotherapy can be a valuable option. These professionals can help uncover the underlying causes of low self-confidence and provide tailored strategies to rebuild and strengthen it.

In the end, self-confidence is a complex and ever-evolving aspect of our lives, influenced by various factors. It's a journey, and seeking guidance and support when needed can make a significant difference in building and maintaining self-confidence. Remember that you are not alone in your quest for self-assurance, and there are resources available to help you along the way.